To the only God of Creativity, the Father, Son, and Holy Spirit.

To Suanne, my wonderful, understanding, helpful wife and friend.

To Lion Players and Fisherpeople Drama Ministry, who breathed life into these vignettes.

Lectionary Scenes

58 Vignettes
For
Cycle B

Robert F. Crowley

CSS Publishing Company, Inc., Lima, Ohio

LECTIONARY SCENES, CYCLE B

Library of Congress Cataloging-in-Publication Data

Crowley, Robert F., 1938-
     Lectionary scenes : 56 vignettes for Cycle C / Robert F. Crowley.
          p.   cm.
     ISBN 0-7880-1060-3 (paperback)
     1. Drama in Christian education. 2. Drama in public worship. 3. Bible plays. 4. Christian drama, American. 5. Common lectionary (1992)   I. Title.
BV289.C76   1997
246'.72—DC21   96-46497
                                                                                      CIP

This book is available in the following formats, listed by ISBN:
     0-7880-1373-4   Book
     0-7880-1374-2   Disk
     0-7880-1375-0   Sermon Prep

Table Of Contents

Preface

For me, the greatest test of a dramatic work is whether the audience reacts to it as the playwright intended. These scenes have passed that test, some of them many times. Members of the audiences who have enjoyed them have requested their favorites over the years. My hope is that when you do them they will be often requested. They are to be enjoyed by actors, directors, and audiences and, I hope, by God.

Introduction

You probably want to act or direct or somehow help produce one or more of these scenes for your church or church-related group. Great! It is possible.

Every human being has the inherent ability to act. God, in His wisdom, created us in His image and therefore we are creative. As actors, directors, or producers of drama, God allows us to co-create with Him. This is a privilege and a responsibility.

Prayer
Talking to God comes first. Do it a lot! Every time there's a snag — pray. Pray as much as you rehearse.

Rehearsal
A lot of rehearsal is necessary for a good performance. A ratio of 40-to-1 is not unreasonable. That means for every minute you are performing you need forty minutes of rehearsal. This does not count memorizing your lines before rehearsal.

Humility
Don't become proud! It is easy for creative people to fall into this trap. Don't let it happen to you. Remember, God used Balaam's donkey to speak for Him. God can use anyone in a drama ministry who is willing to learn and who is obedient.

Awareness
Be alert to the wiles of the Devil. He will attack you before, during, or after the ministry. Pray! Protect yourself. Pray for each other.

Competitiveness

You are not in competition with other members of your troupe. You are their brother or sister in Christ. Treat them as honored members of Jesus' body.

Ministry

Acting these scenes is a ministry, not a performance. The Lord God allows us to minister for Him to others and He also allows us to minister to Him. It is a sacred duty.

God is always teaching me His ways. He will teach you, too. I'm thankful He wants to use all of us. God bless your efforts.

11/30/08

Watch!

Theme

The second advent of Christ and the doctrine of the elect.

Summary

Three Christian friends talk about the second coming of Christ and how it relates to them.

Playing Time	3 minutes
Setting	A church
Props	None
Costumes	Contemporary, casual
Time	The present
Cast	JOYCE
	KAYLA
	CHRISTINA

JOYCE: *(ENTERS ALONG WITH KAYLA AND CHRISTINA)* Well, what do you think?

KAYLA: It all sounds scary to me.

JOYCE: It does a little. "After the tribulation, the sun and moon will be darkened, the stars will fall."

CHRISTINA: Scary and confusing. It sounds to me like the Lord isn't in charge any more.

JOYCE: That can't be true. He's all-powerful and eternal, so he's always in charge and always will be.

KAYLA: Of course, but it does sound like everything is going to be out of control.

JOYCE: This passage is talking about the end of the world as we know it, so it's bound to sound different.

KAYLA: The nice thing about it is, Jesus is there.

CHRISTINA: Not just there. He's actually coming back.

JOYCE: Sure, it's the second advent.

CHRISTINA: The second advent.

KAYLA: What's that mean?

JOYCE: It means he's coming back.

KAYLA: No, I mean "advent," what's that mean?

JOYCE: It means arrival.

KAYLA: He's actually going to be here on earth again?

CHRISTINA: And everyone will see him.

KAYLA: Advent means arrival, and this is talking about his second arrival. Then the first arrival must have been at Bethlehem.

JOYCE: That was it. It was the Son of God's first appearance as a human being.

CHRISTINA: As a baby.

KAYLA: But when he returns he will be seen by everyone.

CHRISTINA: That's exciting. Jesus says it himself. He says he will return in clouds with great power and glory.

KAYLA: But what about the next part, sending angels to gather all the elect?

CHRISTINA: That's us. We're going to be with Jesus.

KAYLA: "Elect!" We're the elect?

JOYCE: That's us.

CHRISTINA: I don't quite get that one myself.

KAYLA: Elect? It must have some deep meaning.

JOYCE: Not too deep, really. It just means chosen. We're chosen to become children of God.

KAYLA: But I wasn't chosen by God. I decided to become his child.

JOYCE: Sure you did. We all did, but God, because he is eternal, is outside time and knew we would choose him. And the Holy Spirit worked in your will so that you would choose him when the time was right.

KAYLA: He actually chose me first. That's nice.

CHRISTINA: He loved us before we loved him.

JOYCE: That's it. He loved us outside of time before we loved him at the right time.

KAYLA: Well, he's coming back for me. That takes away all the fear.

JOYCE: And we'll be together. That's comforting.

CHRISTINA: I'll tell you what, let's keep watching for his arrival. (*EXIT*)

The Boss

Theme

The principle of being humble is not popular and probably never will be, but it is biblical and necessary for God's approval.

Summary

Gus's boss treats him like a slave rather than a person with good ideas. Al, Gus's friend, talks to him about quitting and going elsewhere where he would be appreciated.

Playing Time	3 minutes
Setting	A business setting
Props	None
Costumes	Contemporary, business
Time	The present
Cast	GUS
	AL — his friend

AL: *(AL AND GUS ENTER)* What a meeting! My twelve-year-old could chair a meeting better than that.

GUS: It was a difficult meeting, that's true.

AL: Difficult? I don't see how you stand it. He doesn't let you express your views on anything.

GUS: It's always been like that. I was surprised at first, but I've gotten used to it.

AL: Why don't you do something about it?

GUS: Do something? Like what do you suggest?

AL: Well, quit for one thing.

GUS: No, I don't think the Lord would have me quit my job.

AL: A person of your caliber would certainly be highly sought after.

GUS: I've had offers.

AL: Well?

GUS: I've been praying about it. I'm supposed to be right where I am. Genny agrees.

AL: But your wife doesn't have to put up with your boss like you do.

GUS: That's true. Everything you say is true, but the bottom line is, I am convinced that God gave me this job and he hasn't told me to move yet.

AL: I'd leave just on the principle of the thing.

GUS: I can't do that.

AL: Tell me why.

GUS: I just did.

AL: I know, God put you here, but listen, what does God have to say about your boss being a puffed-up bore?

GUS: He says I should serve him.

AL: You're making that up.

GUS: No, not really.

AL: Where? Where in the Bible does it say that?

GUS: Well, I'll tell you. Paul says that we should be obedient to our masters. (Ephesians 6:5, 6)

AL: I know that passage, but Paul's speaking about slaves.

GUS: It's the same principle. He says that we are slaves of Christ and that we should do the will of God as from the heart.

AL: Now, that's something. Even if we were slaves.

GUS: Right. Some of us are just like slaves in our jobs.

AL: I know.

GUS: Also we're supposed to do our work heartily as for the Lord, rather than men. (Colossians 3:23, 24)

AL: Heartily?

GUS: Yes, put your heart into it.

AL: You sure do that.

GUS: It's the Lord we serve. Not just men.

AL: So, we're not just working for "Mr. Pompous." We're working for the Lord.

GUS: Mainly for the Lord. Our boss is the person the Lord allows to be over us. It's just like what John the Baptist did.

AL: What's that?

GUS: Don't you remember? He said, "He must increase, I must decrease."

AL: Yeah, sure, but he was talking about Jesus, right?

GUS: That's right, but it must be true for every "Master" we have, like our boss. We were hired so the company and the president of the company would be successful. If he's successful, so are we. And we are actually working for the Lord anyway, so we can truly say, "He must increase, I must decrease."

AL: That's tough to do.

GUS: It really is. It must have been tough for John the Baptist, too. He had a great many people following him. And he gave it all up.

AL: So, like John the Baptist, you're going to stay in this job and be a slave to "Mr. Pompous."

GUS: And work as if Jesus were my boss.

AL: You know, I'm going to have to try it.

GUS: But, I'm your boss.

AL: Yeah, well, let's get some coffee. Maybe we can talk about it.

Who Are You?

Theme
Knowing who you are and who you aren't.

Summary
Dan and Ginny talk about their children's future, the careers they will choose, and how their walk with God will affect that.

Playing Time	3 minutes
Setting	Home
Props	None
Costumes	Contemporary, casual
Time	The present
Cast	DAN
	GINNY — his Wife

DAN: (*DAN, GINNY ENTER*) Well, that was some evening, wasn't it?

GINNY: I don't know what those educators are thinking of, wanting young people to decide what their career goals are when they're in junior high school.

DAN: Boy, I almost walked out of the meeting.

GINNY: I'm glad you didn't. They needed to hear your views.

DAN: Well, I guess I gave them a earful.

GINNY: Yes, you did that.

DAN: I'm still angry. Kids have to have time to be kids and not to worry about careers at that age.

GINNY: Johnny and Melissa are certainly kids who are enjoying their youth.

DAN: Good. I mean to help them both get into the right career when the time comes. But that time is not yet.

GINNY: How will we do that?

DAN: Well, I think they have to know who they are first.

GINNY: I think they know who they are. They're not snobbish on the one hand or too intimidated by other people.

DAN: I think you're right.

GINNY: I was just reading about John the Baptist and he seemed to be that way.

DAN: That's right, he was. He knew who he was.

GINNY: And just as importantly, he knew who he wasn't.

DAN: What do you mean?

GINNY: When the officials came to question him and they asked him who he was, the first thing he said was that he was not the Messiah.

DAN: That's interesting. He didn't answer their question about who he was. He told them who he wasn't.

GINNY: Right. It's important to know who you aren't.

DAN: I guess so.

GINNY: Our kids know God and so they won't have any doubts about who they are because God keeps us humble.

DAN: And if they're humble God can use them.

GINNY: And when God puts them to use in his kingdom then they'll be secure in what they are doing.

DAN: God knows our children better than we do, so he will be able to lead them into careers that will fit their personalities exactly. What could be better than that?

GINNY: Nothing, really.

DAN: I feel really secure about our children.

GINNY: Well, we pray for them every day, so God will take care of them.

DAN: Well, c'mon, let's go pray for them while they're sleeping.

GINNY: Good idea.

The Meeting

Theme
Great faith encourages the worship of God.

Summary
Elizabeth, the mother of John the Baptist, meets with Mary, the mother of Jesus, and they encourage each other.

Playing Time	5 minutes
Setting	The house of Elizabeth
Props	None
Costumes	Peasants of Jesus' time
Time	Before the birth of Jesus
Cast	ELIZABETH — the mother of John the Baptist, sixty years old, six months pregnant
	MARY — her cousin, the mother of Jesus, fifteen years old, pregnant

ELIZABETH: (*ENTERS, HUMMING A TUNE AND MENDING A GARMENT*) So many years Zacharias and I have spent waiting on the Lord. Praying and waiting on the Lord. My, my, so many years. I have resigned myself to His will. In my old age I finally realized His wisdom is best.

In my youth I was rebellious. Especially rebellious for the daughter of a priest. But the Lord has redirected my steps to the path He intends for me.

Many years in the process though. But now, praise the Lord God Almighty, He has blessed me with a son. And a mighty child of God he will be, for the Holy messenger of God has promised it and it will surely happen.

26

Oh, Holy God, you know the needs of your children, and your provision is sufficient for us.

MARY: (*CALLING FROM OFFSTAGE*) Elizabeth, my dear cousin, I have wonderful news to share with you.

ELIZABETH: Mary! (*ELIZABETH'S BABY LEAPS IN HER WOMB*) Oh!

MARY: (*ENTERS AND HUGS ELIZABETH, AND THEY BOTH CRY WITH JOY*) Elizabeth! I missed you. I have some marvelous news.

ELIZABETH: Mary, come and sit. (*RAISING HER HANDS IN PRAISE TO GOD*) Glory to the most high God. Mary, you are favored by God and chosen above all other women that ever were and ever shall be. Praise God. When you called to me I knew you carried the promised Messiah, for my own son leaped for joy in my womb. (*SITTING*)

Oh, Mary, you will be blessed. Yes, blessed and happy, and all women will envy you the privilege that has been awarded to you, for you have trusted the Lord and believed that the words He spoke to you are true.

MARY: (*LIFTING HER HANDS IN PRAISE*) Oh, how I praise the Lord. Praises for the Lord come from my innermost being. My soul magnifies the Lord. My spirit rejoices in God, my Savior. For He, the Almighty Holy One, has taken notice of His lowly servant girl and now all generations will call me blessed. His mercy goes on from generation to generation, to all who fear Him. He has satisfied the hungry hearts and exalted the lowly.

He has not forgotten His children, Israel. He will help us and He will be merciful towards us even as He has promised our father, Abraham, and his descendants forever. Praise the Lord for His words to us.

MARY: Remember how I used to tell you every problem? And you always took the time to listen to me? You were so good to me.

ELIZABETH: Of course I listened. You were the child I never had. And I'll listen again, now. Tell me about the Angel Gabriel.

MARY: He frightened me a bit at first but then he said: "Congratulations, you are a woman who is favored by God, chosen by Him above all other women."

He was as bright as the sun at noonday. It hurt my eyes to look at him, but I couldn't turn away either. He smiled gently at me.

"Don't be afraid," he said. And he called me by my name. "For you have found absolute favor and loving kindness with God."

His voice was great. I was sure the entire village must have shaken at the sound of it, but it was clear and melodic like the instruments they play in the temple.

And then he told me the most marvelous thing. He said: "Now listen to me carefully. Very soon now you will become pregnant and will give birth to a son." And then he said that I should name my son "Yeshuah."

Then he told me that my son will be very great and will be called the very Son of the Most High. And he said the Lord God Himself will give the throne of David to Him. He said that my son will reign over Israel forever and that His kingdom will never end.

Well, I didn't understand it all. I still don't. I asked how all this he said could happen, since I have never known a man.

He said that God's own Holy Spirit would come upon me and the power of the Holy Spirit would overshadow me so that the son borne by me would be pure and sinless and utterly Holy — the Son of God.

Then with a booming voice that seemed to shake the earth, he said: "With God nothing is ever impossible and no word from God shall be without power or impossible of fulfillment."

Well, with that my fear was gone as if the wind blew it out of my soul. I found a peace in my heart. I told the angel: "I am the Lord's servant and I am willing to obey Him and do whatever He wants. May everything you said come to pass."

Then he was gone. In a second he just vanished, but I shall never forget him. Never. What happened next was more glorious. The power of the Spirit.

I felt as if I were in some other place, some place of love, a place where I was completely loved. Such a feeling of peace overwhelmed me. It was over in a moment. But I knew from that ecstatic moment of joy that I carried the promise of God beneath my heart.

Never will I forget it. I never want to, for someday I may need the strength and power and faith the Lord of Hosts gave me in that wonderful moment.

ELIZABETH: Oh, praise the Most High God. Oh, great Lord, forever and ever you have been with us. You care for your chosen people. Great is the Lord. Great is your wisdom.

Now, oh, Lord, you have fulfilled your promise to us. You have sent us your Son, the Messiah, the Chosen One. Praise you, Yahweh. Praise to you, Yeshuah, the Messiah. Praise to you, Holy Spirit of God.

The Birthday

Theme

The Holy Spirit works to bring everyone to Jesus.

Summary

Mary, the mother of Jesus, and John, the beloved disciple, have opened their home to a friendless girl, Tirzah, whose background, when she compares it to the Christian life, as the Master lived it, was lively. After listening to Mary recount the story of Jesus' birth, as only a mother can tell it, Tirzah accepts the new way of life and becomes a Christian.

Playing Time	8 minutes
Setting	The house of John
Props	Stools, bowls, cups, pitcher
Costumes	Peasants of Jesus' time
Time	After the resurrection of Jesus
Cast	MARY — the mother of Jesus
	JOHN — the beloved disciple of Jesus
	TIRZAH — a young girl of the streets

(MARY IS SEATED CENTER STAGE ON A LOW STOOL MEND-ING SOME GARMENTS AND SINGING SOFTLY TO HERSELF)

TIRZAH: *(OFFSTAGE)* The meal will soon be ready.

MARY: Good. John said he would return early tonight.

TIRZAH: (*ENTERS CARRYING A BOWL AND STIRRING SOME CURDS*) Where did he go today?

MARY: He said he was going to stay in the city.

TIRZAH: (*KNEELING BESIDE MARY*) May we eat with him tonight?

MARY: I'll ask.

TIRZAH: There will be no visitors tonight.

MARY: As far as we know. There's no telling who John will bring home with him.

TIRZAH: They're usually very nice people but a little dull.

MARY: He brought you home.

TIRZAH: And I am thankful. This is a nice home and I'm grateful John took me in.

MARY: John is like that. His heart is full of love. He's always bringing someone home for a meal or to stay the night or sometimes even longer. He took me in. Many years ago, when Jesus was arrested, I had no one to care for me ...

TIRZAH: I'll bet John found you on the street like he did me.

MARY: Well, no, not quite. Remember, I told you, Jesus ...

TIRZAH: The Messiah, your son.

MARY: Yes, that's right. Jesus was the sacrifice so that everyone can live forever with the heavenly Father.

TIRZAH: Yes, I remember.

MARY: As Jesus was hanging on the cross making that sacrifice he had so much compassion for me, his mother, that he told John to care for me.

TIRZAH: Why did he choose John?

MARY: I think he chose John because John has a great capacity to love and also because Jesus loves John dearly. John has been very good to me. You'll be well taken care of.

TIRZAH: I've been working for it.

MARY: Yes, we all do what we can. You should thank the Lord that you're healthy and can do the work.

TIRZAH: I've always worked, ever since I can remember.

MARY: But this is honest work.

TIRZAH: And hard.

MARY: It's good for you. Don't you feel better than you did when you first came here?

TIRZAH: Better? Well, I suppose I do, a little. But I miss the gaiety, the parties, the fine clothing, the good food, and the exciting people.

MARY: And the sickness.

TIRZAH: No, I don't miss that.

MARY: The Lord has really strengthened your body.

TIRZAH: And I'm glad. I really am, but I miss the fun.

(JOHN ENTERS BUT TIRZAH DOES NOT SEE HIM)

MARY: What you were doing couldn't have been fun.

TIRZAH: It was and I miss it.

JOHN: *(REMOVING HIS CLOAK)* What do you miss, Tirzah? *(KISSING MARY)* Good evening, Mary.

TIRZAH: I miss having a good time.

JOHN: When I found you, you weren't having such a good time.

TIRZAH: Yes, I know, but there were good days, before the sickness came.

JOHN: Don't ever forget how you got the sickness.

TIRZAH: But, I've been cured. I know it.

JOHN: Not completely, I guess.

TIRZAH: I have. I'm as healthy as anyone.

JOHN: Your body has been healed. We'll await the rest. But, enough of this. Let's eat. I'm famished. *(SITTING. TIRZAH SILENTLY SIGNALS MARY)*

MARY: John, Tirzah wants to know if we may eat with you tonight.

JOHN: Yes. We're having no guests tonight. Of course you may.

TIRZAH: *(EXITING)* Oh, thank you, thank you. I'll bring the food.

(MARY OFFERS JOHN A BOWL. HE WASHES HIS HANDS AND SO DOES MARY.)

JOHN: It might cheer her.

MARY: That's why I asked.

JOHN: Has she been like this long?

MARY: A couple of days.

JOHN: I'm afraid I hadn't noticed.

MARY: It comes and goes. She has a lot to forget.

(*TIRZAH ENTERS WITH BREAD, WINE, AND CURDS*)

JOHN: (*LIFTING THE BREAD FOR A BLESSING*) For those who gave us the bread, we ask a blessing. Bless the Lord who provided for them and through them, us. (*LIFTING THE WINE*) A blessing on you, First Born of the Dead. Feed us with your food and drink. (*THEY EAT*)

MARY: How was your day?

JOHN: An exciting day, but then they all are.

MARY: Nothing special?

JOHN: Yes, there was something. I talked to Joasar, the Pharisee.

MARY: And did he understand?

JOHN: Better than that, he accepted.

MARY: Bless the Lord. May his name be praised forever. You've been talking to him a long time.

JOHN: Yes, a long time. Since Pentecost.

MARY: Has it really been that long? It seems like only yesterday.

JOHN: Yes, it does. It's strange. Joasar was there at Pentecost, I mean, after we were all touched by the Holy Spirit of God. He heard Peter's message but just couldn't accept Jesus as Messiah and Lord of his life. Now he has. It took seventeen years. Finally he accepted the truth. The others will make it difficult for him. When a Pharisee believes on the Messiah they won't even let him buy anything in the streets.

MARY: But now he has someone to carry his load.

TIRZAH: Someone to carry his load?

MARY: Jesus.

TIRZAH: Oh.

JOHN: He'll be all right. He's going to come to our meetings. He'll find new friends soon and the believers will support him.

TIRZAH: All this talk of help and support and someone to carry the load; it tires me just to listen. Please, could you tell us a story, John? Anything to pass the time. The nights are so dull and boring with so little to do.

MARY: A story would be nice, John.

TIRZAH: The days are so busy. Why can't we have some fun? Don't you people ever have any fun?

JOHN: Fun? Yes, lots of it.

TIRZAH: Is that bad, to want some fun?

JOHN: No, not bad. That sounds really good to me, too.

TIRZAH: It does?

JOHN: I miss the good times. There's so much work to do that I forget that we need to relax sometimes and just have fun.

TIRZAH: Do you mean parties? I didn't think you people ever had parties.

MARY: Oh, yes. You just haven't been here long enough. We've had some exciting parties, and we will again.

JOHN: And very soon, too. Two of our group are getting married.

TIRZAH: Did the Messiah ever attend a party?

MARY: Why, of course.

JOHN: It was at a wedding party that he performed his first miracle.

TIRZAH: Tell us.

JOHN: It was the first time we ever saw anything like that. And then, when we'd seen it, we weren't sure what we saw.

TIRZAH: What did he do? What happened?

JOHN: The wedding feast was so much fun no one noticed until it was too late that we were running out of wine.

MARY: So I told the servants to follow the orders of Jesus and he simply told them to fill the water pots with water.

JOHN: And when a cup of it was tasted, we found it was wine, and good wine too.

MARY: As I recall, no one went home that night.

JOHN: The party lasted three days and it was such a fine celebration.

MARY: John, do you remember how we used to celebrate each other's birthdays?

TIRZAH: Birthdays?

JOHN: Of course I remember. None of us had ever done it before. Whose idea was that, anyway?

MARY: Jesus', I think. Yes, I'm sure it was his idea.

JOHN: Those were joyful occasions.

TIRZAH: How do you celebrate a birthday and why?

JOHN: Why? I couldn't figure that out myself, at first. I thought, why would anyone want to celebrate being born? It's painful for both mother and child.

MARY: But what a joyful pain.

JOHN: But I learned that being born is the only way we can have life, and a second birth is necessary if we want to have a glorious and everlasting life.

TIRZAH: But how?

JOHN: Well, you have to accept the Messiah as the Son of God and a Lord of your life.

TIRZAH: No, I mean at the celebration, what did you do?

JOHN: Oh.

MARY: We had a party.

JOHN: And what a party. Every year, on the same day, we'd have a party for the person who was born on that day.

MARY: And it was a special day. He was treated as an honored guest all day.

JOHN: We'd have sweet cakes.

TIRZAH: But I don't even know on what day I was born.

MARY: Many of us didn't either, so those who didn't each chose a day on which to celebrate their birth. Some of us chose the date of our second birth.

TIRZAH: It sounds wonderful.

JOHN: It is. After the feast we'd sing and dance and tell stories.

MARY: We all danced, even the older ones. Of course the younger ones were the best, but we all danced a little.

JOHN: A lot of people complained about our parties, but Jesus told them that we should be celebrating while he was here with us because the time would come when he wouldn't be with us.

TIRZAH: Who told the stories?

JOHN: There were some who were better storytellers, but most of us were pretty big talkers. Anyway, I think Jesus, Philip, Matthew, Nicodemas, and of course Mary here, were the best storytellers.

MARY: You were good yourself, John.

JOHN: I was a better listener, I think. I loved to hear Jesus tell stories. All his stories had some meaning for us.

TIRZAH: Which was your favorite?

JOHN: My favorite? Hmm, let's see. Well, strangely enough, it wasn't one that Jesus told, but it was about him. I always wanted to hear Mary tell of Jesus' birth.

TIRZAH: Please tell it now, Mary. I always wanted to hear about Jesus' birth.

JOHN: Mary?

MARY: It was so glorious. My husband and I left our home in Nazareth and traveled to Bethlehem in Judea. It was for the census ordered by the Roman government.

Joseph could have gone alone, but after talking it over and praying about it we decided it would be best for us both to go. He sold half his tools to buy a donkey to carry me on the long journey. She was a dear animal. We called her Vashni, the strong one.

It was too uncomfortable a trip considering my condition; it was a long one. We traveled across the plain of Esdraelon, down the Jordan River valley to Jericho, then up to Jerusalem and then to Bethlehem. As we approached the town I knew my time was near.

It was late afternoon and the streets were still crowded with people, mostly travelers like us. Joseph could find no place to lodge us. He was desperate and I was concerned with my pain and wasn't much help to him. So, we prayed together, and then Joseph got the idea of staying in one of the caverns in the hillsides in which animals were kept during the cool of the year.

It was a dark and damp place, but I knew in my heart that my firstborn was special, for no man had known me. It was a miracle. God had touched me.

While I prepared myself I thought back to the visit from the glorious messenger from the Lord of Heaven, how he told me it would happen. But when the spirit of God came upon me, I can hardly explain it, it was almost joyfully unbearable. From that time I knew a new life grew strong inside my womb. And I knew it was he of whom all the prophets speak. I knew it was the Messiah, the Chosen one, the Son of God.

I was alone with my thoughts and my pain. Joseph was nearby, but of course was not allowed to help with the birth. I could hear him outside, walking back and forth, praying and saying encouraging things to me.

The pain was intense, but I delivered quickly, and the moment I saw him and held him and cleaned his little body I knew it would have been worth much more pain.

He was so pretty, his eyes so dark that the contrast between the dark and the light of them seemed a place to jump off into the soul of him. Everyone who saw him remarked about his eyes. He had a lot more hair than most newly born babies and it was curly. His lips were a dark rose color and his skin was dark, too, like the color of wheat bread. His little hands were so fine, so beautiful, but he was a large child, long, so we knew he was going to be tall. And when he slept we could see him breathe and it was a most wondrous miracle to know that this baby was a gift from our Creator.

JOHN: I never tire of that story.

TIRZAH: I love it too. I would have loved to meet him.

MARY: Good. You shall.

TIRZAH: How?

JOHN: By doing as we all did; realizing who he is ...

TIRZAH: But I already know — the Son of God.

JOHN: ... And telling him you want him to direct your life.

TIRZAH: Oh, I do want that.

MARY: Let's do it.

TIRZAH: But, how do I do it?

JOHN: Just ask him.

TIRZAH: Like he was here?

JOHN: He is.

TIRZAH: All right. Dear Messiah, I know who you are. Take control of my life. I haven't done so well with it. How was that?

JOHN: That's good enough. Now you're completely healed.

TIRZAH: I feel so clean.

MARY: You really are now.

TIRZAH: I see everything more clearly. I feel so good and clean. Oh, I've got a good idea. Let's celebrate the Messiah's birthday every year and tell stories about him and sing and treat him as the honored guest just as if he were here with us, physically, I mean.

JOHN: Yes, I think that would please him.

MARY: I'm sure it does. (*THEY ALL EXIT JOYFULLY*)

Money Business

Theme
Giving to others is the real spirit of Christmas.

Summary
Three "lucky" people find a deposit bag full of money and decide to split it among them. They then decide the best thing to do is give the money away.

Playing Time	3 minutes
Setting	A mall at Christmastime
Props	A Salvation Army kettle, bank deposit bag, necklace
Costumes	Appropriate for Christmas shopping
Time	The present
Cast	SALVATION ARMY VOLUNTEER
	WOMAN
	BOYFRIEND
	MARLENE — a hair stylist on her lunch break
	BILL — a teenager with time to waste
	GEORGE — a carpenter in a hurry to get home and watch the game

(A WOMAN CARRYING A BANK DEPOSIT BAG FILLED WITH MONEY HURRIES TO THE BANK BUT SEES HER BOYFRIEND AND STOPS TO HUG AND TALK TO HIM. HE PRESENTS HER WITH A NECKLACE AND SHE PUTS THE BAG DOWN ON A BENCH TO PUT ON THE NECKLACE. MARLENE, GEORGE, AND BILL ENTER, EACH GOING DIFFERENT WAYS. THEY

42

*SEE THE BAG AND REACH FOR IT. SINCE THEY ARE LOOK-
ING AROUND TO SEE IF THEY ARE BEING WATCHED THEY
DON'T SEE THE TWO OTHER HANDS ON THE BAG.)*

MARLENE: Hey! This is mine. I found it.

BILL: I had my hand on it first.

GEORGE: *(WRENCHING IT OUT OF THEIR HANDS)* I guess
I have it now.

MARLENE: What about finders-keepers?

GEORGE: What about grabbies-havvies? *(OPENS THE BAG
AND TAKES OUT MONEY)*

BILL: There's enough for all of us. We can split it three ways.

GEORGE: I don't know.

MARLENE: I guess it's all right. One third's better than nothing.
(SHE DIVIDES IT EVENLY)

BILL: Wow!

GEORGE: And how!

MARLENE: It certainly is a lot of money.

BILL: Okay, see ya. *(BEGINS TO EXIT)*

MARLENE: Wait! I feel sort of funny — taking this money like
this.

GEORGE: I have a family — three kids and a wife. I didn't know
how I was going to afford Christmas presents this year. This will
do it.

MARLENE: Christmas presents? You could buy the entire mall with this much money.

BILL: So, what do you suggest, we take it back? We don't even know where it came from.

MARLENE: I just want to give it back.

GEORGE: We don't know where it came from.

MARLENE: Then we should just turn it over to the security and let them handle it.

GEORGE: Why don't you just hand over your share?

BILL: We can't let her do that. They'll find out it's only one third of it. Then she'll tell them about us. I'm outta here.

GEORGE: Wait! I don't want to get in trouble. Let's decide what we're going to do about the money and do it together.

MARLENE: I say we give it to security.

GEORGE: I say we keep it.

BILL: Yeah, keep it. Let's get out of here before someone becomes suspicious.

MARLENE: I've got a better idea. Let's give it all away.

GEORGE: What!

BILL: No way.

MARLENE: Look, I need this money as much as either of you, but did you ever think of all the poor people who are worse off than we are?

BILL: No, not really.

GEORGE: I gave to the United Campaign.

MARLENE: Well, here's your chance to give in a big way.

BILL: Well, it would be nice to help the homeless.

GEORGE: I guess my kids have all the toys they need. Yeah, we could do it.

MARLENE: All right. Let's all put out money back in the bag and then we'll put it in that kettle over there.

GEORGE: Let's do it before I change my mind. (*THEY PUT THE MONEY BACK IN THE BAG AND ALL THREE PLACE IT IN THE KETTLE.*)

MARLENE: There, now, don't you feel better?

BILL: I feel poorer.

MARLENE: It does feel good to give at Christmas.

(*AS THEY BEGIN TO EXIT THEIR SEVERAL WAYS THE WOMAN WHO LAID THE BAG DOWN RETURNS AND SEES IT ON THE KETTLE. SHE HURRIES OVER AND GRABS IT, THANKS THE SALVATION ARMY VOLUNTEER BUT BEFORE SHE LEAVES SHE DROPS SOME MONEY IN THE KETTLE. MARLENE, GEORGE, AND BILL SEE THIS AND RETURN TO DROP MONEY IN THE KETTLE AND THEN EXIT.*)

1/29/12

Making A Christian

Theme

Depending on the leading of the Holy Spirit is better than some pattern.

Summary

Sam is telling Bill how to evangelize and forces him to do some unnatural things. Amazingly there is some fruit.

Playing Time	4 minutes
Setting	Anywhere
Props	None
Costumes	Contemporary, casual
Time	The present
Cast	SAM
	BILL
	WILL

SAM: (*SAM AND BILL ENTER*) Are you a Christian?

BILL: Yes. I am.

SAM: Get anybody born again yet?

BILL: Well, no. I haven't. I'm not so good ...

SAM: Not so good at that, are you?

BILL: Well, no. I guess I'm not.

SAM: I'm not surprised. Look at you.

BILL: What? What's wrong?

SAM: Look at that!

BILL: What? What are you talking about?

SAM: I'm talking about your face.

BILL: My face? You don't like my face?

SAM: It's not a question of whether I like it or not.

BILL: Oh? What is it a question of?

SAM: Why, my dear man, it's a question of whether you look like a Christian or not.

BILL: It is?

SAM: Why, yes, of course it is.

BILL: And I don't look like a Christian?

SAM: Almost, but not quite.

BILL: I don't, eh?

SAM: No, you don't.

BILL: Well, how does a Christian look?

SAM: A Christian looks ... intense.

BILL: (*WITH AN EXAGGERATED LOOK OF INTENSITY*) How's this?

SAM: Well, not bad.

BILL: More? (*EVEN MORE INTENSE*)

SAM: There, that's about it. Now, hold that look.

BILL: Do I have it?

SAM: Naw, you'll never make it.

BILL: What? What is it now?

SAM: You don't know any scripture, do you?

BILL: Well, no, I don't, but I could learn.

SAM: Maybe.

BILL: No, really, I could.

SAM: I don't know.

BILL: Teach me one.

SAM: Well, all right. How about this one: "After me comes one who is mightier than I, and I am not even fit to stoop down and untie the thong of his sandals."

BILL: I have to learn that whole thing?

SAM: Yes. You have to learn scripture if you want to get people born again.

BILL: All right. I'll work on it. "After me comes one ..."

SAM: You're looking pretty good.

BILL: Not real good yet, huh?

SAM: Needs a little work.

BILL: "After ..." Uh.

SAM: "ME! AFTER ME!"

BILL: I've got it. "After me ..." Uh.

SAM: "COMES ONE!" "COMES ONE!"

BILL: "Comes one."

SAM: "AFTER! — ME! — COMES! — ONE!"

BILL: I've got it now. "After me comes one."

SAM: "WHO! — IS! — MIGHTIER! — THAN! — I!"

BILL: "Who is mightier than I."

SAM: You have to say it with conviction.

BILL: I have to act like I mean it.

SAM: Right you are.

BILL: (*LOUDLY*) "ONE IS COMING."

SAM: No, not "one is coming." It's: "After me comes one."

BILL: I've got it. "After me comes one."

SAM: Yes, not bad. You're getting there. Now, a little lower.

BILL: (*BENDING OVER*) "After me ..."

49

SAM: No, no. The pitch. Lower the pitch. (*DEMONSTRATING WITH A LOW TONE*) "After me comes one."

BILL: I get it. (*IN A LOW TONE*) "After me comes one."

SAM: Much better. Keep it right there.

BILL: (*EVERYTHING WITH A LOW TONE*) Am I ready yet?

SAM: Pretty much. One thing though.

BILL: What one thing?

SAM: You've got to be more spiritual. Here, fold your hands like this. (*AN EXAGGERATED PRAYER POSTURE*)

BILL: (*FOLLOWING TEACHER*) I've got it.

SAM: Good. Perfect. Now you're ready.

BILL: I am?

SAM: Yes, of course.

BILL: Well, I do feel different.

SAM: Believe me, you look different too.

BILL: Now what do I do?

SAM: Go harvest a crop.

BILL: Harvest?

SAM: Why, yes, of course. You're ready. Go witness your faith.

BILL: Where do I go?

SAM: Out in the highways and byways of life. Don't you listen to the sermons?

BILL: Do I have to start doing that too?

SAM: You certainly do. Where do you think I got all my knowledge?

BILL: I never thought about it.

SAM: And that's another thing. You must stop thinking.

BILL: Maybe I could just cut down a little.

SAM: Hey, do you want to ruin everything? Don't think. Just be moved to do things. That's the way I do it.

BILL: I get it.

SAM: Good. I think you're ready.

BILL: Really? (*WILL ENTERS*)

SAM: Yes. Now, go get that person born again.

BILL: (*WALKING UP TO WILL*) "SOME GUY IS COMING AFTER ME!"

WILL: Huh?

BILL: Uh ... "HE'S BIGGER THAN I AM ..."

WILL: What's with you?

BILL: Uh ... "AND I CAN'T EVEN BEND DOWN ..."

WILL: Are you well?

BILL: Uh, yeah, I guess so.

WILL: Good. (*BEGINS TO EXIT*)

BILL: Hey, wait! You don't want to be born again, do you?

WILL: Yeah, I guess I do.

BILL: You do?

WILL: Sure. What do I have to do?

BILL: Well, uh, I don't know. I didn't learn that yet. Wait right here. (*CROSSING TO SAM*) What do I do? I think he's ready to harvest.

SAM: Good. Good.

BILL: Well, what do I do?

SAM: Go ask him if he wants to give his heart to Jesus.

BILL: (*CROSSING TO WILL*) Are you still sure you want to do this?

WILL: Yes, I guess so.

BILL: Good. Give your heart to Jesus.

WILL: Okay.

BILL: Good. You're a Christian. Now, go out and get someone born again.

WILL: How do I do that?

BILL: Well, first off you have to look intense, like I do.

WILL: I can do that. (*WILL AND BILL EXIT*)

SAM: Can you beat that. I had fantastic success and that's the first time I ever told anyone how to do that.

The Chosen One

Theme
The call to follow Jesus is not without difficulty.

Summary
Jesus calls Nathanael to be a disciple but Nathanael is also listening to two other voices — one encouraging him to respond and the other discouraging him.

Playing Time	3 minutes
Setting	A neutral playing area
Props	None
Costumes	Contemporary, casual; Jesus in robe
Time	The present
Cast	JESUS
	DISTURBING ANGEL
	MINISTERING ANGEL
	NATHANAEL

JESUS: (*ENTERS AND CROSSES TO NATHANAEL*) Nathanael, follow me.

DISTURBING ANGEL: (*ENTERS AND CROSSES BEHIND NATHANAEL*) Pay no attention to him. He probably wants to sell you something. Or he wants you to commit some time to a project. You've done this before. What's it got you? Nothing! Pass him by. Act like you didn't hear him.

MINISTERING ANGEL: (*ENTERS AND CROSSES BEHIND NATHANAEL*) This is the person you've been studying about, the Messiah, the Chosen One.

DISTURBING ANGEL: How can you be sure he's the one? If you follow him you might get in a lot of trouble with the religious authorities.

MINISTERING ANGEL: But just think if it, if he is the one he might teach you things about God and a relationship with God. That would be worth the risk, wouldn't it?

DISTURBING ANGEL: Risk is a good appraisal of this situation. You have a family to think of. What happens to them if you go off somewhere with this man doing who knows what?

MINISTERING ANGEL: You've been studying what Moses and the prophets have said about him. What do you remember about what you studied?

NATHANAEL: I remember something out of the book of Job. "Oh, that I knew where I might find Him."

MINISTERING ANGEL: Good. Good. You have wanted to talk to God, haven't you? Well, here's your chance.

DISTURBING ANGEL: Oh, that's good. You want to talk to God. Do you know what people will say about you if they even get a hint that you "talk to God"? You're going to lose all your friends. You don't have that many friends that you can afford to lose any.

MINISTERING ANGEL: But what if this man is the "friend that sticks closer than a brother"?

NATHANAEL: "There is a friend that sticks closer than a brother."

MINISTERING ANGEL: Yes. Remember that. Here is that friend, Jesus of Nazareth.

NATHANAEL: Yes, I believe it might be. But Nazareth! Can anything good come from there?

DISTURBING ANGEL: I couldn't have said it better myself. Don't you think Philip is overreacting? He tends to do that. You need to stay away from this guy. He could get you into something you don't want to be in. You could get in trouble with the religious authorities.

MINISTERING ANGEL: But what about Philip? Remember, he said, "Come and see." Now, there's a friend who cares about you. You can trust Philip. He has found the Messiah and you're the first person he shared that news with. You know he loves you.

DISTURBING ANGEL: Don't you wonder why Philip says, "Come and see"? If he really cared that much about you why doesn't he ever explain anything to you? No, he just says, "Come and see." And he expects you to follow like some dog following his master.

MINISTERING ANGEL: Now, listen, has Philip been a friend or not? Didn't you study the scriptures together? You've had some great discussions about the Messiah. Aren't you the least bit interested in who this Jesus is?

JESUS: Here is an honest man. A true son of Israel.

NATHANAEL: How do you know me or what I'm like?

DISTURBING ANGEL: That's right. This may be a trap. Has your "friend" Philip been talking behind your back? Watch yourself.

MINISTERING ANGEL: If they've been talking behind your back it must have been all good things. Jesus only said true things to you. This is the Messiah. The Chosen One. Listen to him.

JESUS: When you were under the fig tree I saw you. Before Philip called you.

DISTURBING ANGEL: Oh, this is too much. This is spooky stuff. You better get out of here. This guy is some kind of weird guy.

MINISTERING ANGEL: Aren't you interested in someone who had so much interest in you? There were a lot of people around today when Jesus passed by. He could only have picked you out of the crowd if he was the Son of God.

NATHANAEL: Teacher, you are truly the son of God and the King of Israel.

JESUS: Do you believe all this just because I told you I had seen you under the fig tree? You will see greater proofs than that. You will even see heaven open and the angels of God coming back and forth to me, the Messiah.

DISTURBING ANGEL: This is really getting out of hand. You're an intelligent man. Do you really think he wants people to take him seriously?

NATHANAEL: Wait a minute! I believe him. Get out of here.

DISTURBING ANGEL: Now, that's no way to talk to an old friend. I was trying to talk some sense into the situation. Now, listen to me.

NATHANAEL: No! I'm not going to listen to you anymore.

DISTURBING ANGEL: Now, wait a minute. You have taken some good sound advice from me in the past and I intend to stay around just to protect you from this man. What he says is disturbing.

JESUS: Absolutely not! Now, you just leave. (*DISTURBING ANGEL BEGINS TO COMPLAIN*) Not a word. Just leave. (*DIS-TURBING ANGEL EXITS*)

MINISTERING ANGEL: Praise to you, Jesus. You are the victorious one. (*MINISTERING ANGEL CONTINUES TO PRAISE AS ALL EXIT*)

1/22/12   4/25/09

By Thunder

Theme
What is it that makes people follow Jesus?

Summary
Zebedee wonders why his sons are following Jesus.

Playing Time	3 1/2 minutes
Setting	The home of Zebedee
Props	None
Costumes	Peasants of Jesus' time
Time	The time of Jesus
Cast	ZEBEDEE — a businessman who owns a fishing business MIRIAMNE — his wife

ZEBEDEE: (*ENTERS*) Miriamne, It's me.

MIRIAMNE: (*ENTERS, DRYING HER HANDS ON A TOWEL*) You're a little late.

ZEBEDEE: Late! It's a wonder I made it home at all.

MIRIAMNE: Why? What happened?

ZEBEDEE: Aw, it's those boys. I don't know what I'm going to do, that's all.

MIRIAMNE: Slow down. Relax. Tell me all about it.

ZEBEDEE: Relax, she says. I can't relax. Aw, those boys.

MIRIAMNE: What? What did they do?

ZEBEDEE: Do? They're gone.

MIRIAMNE: What do you mean "gone"?

ZEBEDEE: Gone. They're gone.

MIRIAMNE: They're gone? Well, they'll be back.

ZEBEDEE: They won't be back. They're gone. Gone!

MIRIAMNE: What are you talking about?

ZEBEDEE: *(EXASPERATED)* I don't know — you try to bring them up right and then you find out they're fanatics.

MIRIAMNE: They do take after you.

ZEBEDEE: Me? I'm no fanatic.

MIRIAMNE: To other people you probably seem like a fanatic.

ZEBEDEE: Me? Me? What are you talking about?

MIRIAMNE: Well, you do go to the synagogue every day.

ZEBEDEE: As all good people of the covenant should.

MIRIAMNE: But how many do?

ZEBEDEE: *(ENTHUSIASTICALLY)* Not enough. That's for sure. Not as many as should. Where else can we read God's precious word? Nowhere else. "Thy word have I hid in my heart that I might not sin against thee." You can't know the word of God unless you go to the synagogue to hear it.

MIRIAMNE: You see what I mean? Others would probably think you are a fanatic.

ZEBEDEE: Because I love the word of God? Everyone should be such a fanatic.

MIRIAMNE: Maybe. But you can't expect your sons to be any different.

ZEBEDEE: Sure, they love the word of God, but this is different.

MIRIAMNE: For goodness' sake, Zeb, what did James and John do?

ZEBEDEE: I already told you. They left. They're gone.

MIRIAMNE: Where? Where did they go?

ZEBEDEE: Well, here's what happened — we were just spreading out our nets, after a very good night, I might add ...

MIRIAMNE: Oh, good. Good. You caught a lot of fish.

ZEBEDEE: Yes, yes, a good catch. We were just getting the nets spread out and along comes Jesus.

MIRIAMNE: Jesus?

ZEBEDEE: Yes, you know. The one we've heard so much about. From Nazareth.

MIRIAMNE: Oh, sure. The boys have been talking about him.

ZEBEDEE: Well, Jesus comes along and says something to them and they both just dropped their nets and followed him.

MIRIAMNE: You're joking.

ZEBEDEE: Joking! I wish I were joking. No. They just dropped their nets and followed him.

MIRIAMNE: My goodness.

ZEBEDEE: I saw what happened and jumped out of the boat and ran after them telling them to get back to work.

MIRIAMNE: And did they finish their work?

ZEBEDEE: No. They didn't. That's why I'm late. They just left me there with the boat and the hired servants. Can you believe it?

MIRIAMNE: Barely. You had to lay out the nets yourself?

ZEBEDEE: I sure did. Can you believe it? Just walked away. Left their old father to do the work.

MIRIAMNE: Where will they live? What will they eat?

ZEBEDEE: How will *we* eat, is a better question. The ungrateful young ...

MIRIAMNE: Neither one of them had a cloak with him. How will they keep warm when the evening chill comes?

ZEBEDEE: Let them freeze. Imagine, it took me two extra hours to get those nets laid out. Two extra hours!

MIRIAMNE: What was it Jesus said to them?

ZEBEDEE: He said, "Follow me and I will make you become fishers of men."

MIRIAMNE: Fishers of men? What does that mean?

ZEBEDEE: I don't know. It doesn't make sense to me.

MIRIAMNE: Fishers of men.

ZEBEDEE: I spent my whole life teaching them to be fishers of *fish.*

MIRIAMNE: Fishers of men. Fishers of men.

ZEBEDEE: Will you stop saying that.

MIRIAMNE: Fishers of men.

ZEBEDEE: Yes, fishers of men. Why would anyone fish for men?

MIRIAMNE: Fishers of men. Maybe Jesus wants them to ask people to follow him, as he asked them to do. Like fishing for fish, but for men.

ZEBEDEE: What in the world am I going to do tomorrow? Where am I going to get two men who work as well as James and John? They just walked off. All Jesus has to do is ask people to follow him and they do. What a crazy world. If everyone left his work and followed Jesus, who would work? What would happen to the world? Who does he think he is?

MIRIAMNE: The Messiah?

ZEBEDEE: Yeah, who does he think he is, the Messiah?

MIRIAMNE and ZEBEDEE: The Messiah!

MIRIAMNE: What if he is the Messiah?

ZEBEDEE: What do you mean, "What if he is the Messiah?" You should see him. He's just a carpenter. Just a carpenter, not the Messiah.

MIRIAMNE: What should the Messiah look like?

ZEBEDEE: I don't know, but not like this guy.

MIRIAMNE: Fishers of men.

ZEBEDEE: Stop saying "fishers of men." The Messiah wouldn't say "fishers of men." Men wouldn't just get up and leave their father to do all the work. The Messiah wouldn't ask people to leave their work.

MIRIAMNE: Fishers of men. Fishers of men.

ZEBEDEE: Will you please stop saying that.

MIRIAMNE: Fishers of men.

ZEBEDEE: Stop it! All right, fishers of men. Hmm. What if he is the Messiah? I guess the Messiah could do anything he wanted to do. If he wants to teach my boys to be fishers of men he couldn't have picked better men to do it. I trained them, didn't I? He knew the best when he saw them.

MIRIAMNE: What will you do tomorrow — about the fishing?

ZEBEDEE: The fishing? Aw, don't worry so much. The fishing will take care of itself. The fish will always be there, won't they? The Lord sees to that. What's important is that my sons have been chosen to learn from the Messiah. My sons!

MIRIAMNE: Yes, but what if he is not the Messiah?

ZEBEDEE: What do you mean? Of course he's the Messiah. Who else could make men leave their life's work and follow him?

MIRIAMNE: What are you saying?

ZEBEDEE: Fishing for fish? I can train anyone to do that job. But fishing for men — only the Messiah could train men for that job. Fishers of men. If I was younger I could do that job. I could fish for some men. I'd show them. I'd bring in a big catch of men. Boy, if I was younger.

Demon Drop

Theme

There are evil forces at work trying to destroy all that is good and trying to destroy God's people as well.

Summary

The Dark Lord is angry because a religious demon has failed, but the demon has a plan to trap the Holy One of Israel — Jesus.

Playing Time	3 minutes
Setting	The throne room of the Dark Lord
Props	Throne
Costumes	Black hooded robes
Time	The time of Jesus
Cast	DARK LORD
	NIGITH — his underling
	GUARDS

DARK LORD: Bring in the accused. (*TWO GUARDS FORCE-FULLY DRAG IN A PITIFUL FORM. IT COWERS IN FRONT OF THE DARK LORD'S THRONE*) What are you doing back here?

NIGITH: It's not my fault, my prince.

DARK LORD: When you fail it is always your fault. And you failed, you whimpering, thoughtless sloth.

NIGITH: He sent me back here. I couldn't help it.

DARK LORD: Silence! Your screeching, rasping voice violates my ears. When you fail your fate is sealed. Guards, take this thing out of my sight. Out of my sight! Dispose of it. I can't stand to look at it any longer. *(GUARDS START TO LEAD NIGITH OUT)*

NIGITH: No-o-o. Listen to me. I still have a plan. I know how to deal with the Holy One of God.

DARK LORD: Do not speak his name before me.

NIGITH: *(BREAKS AWAY FROM THE GUARDS AND RETURNS TO FACE THE DARK LORD.)* Listen to me, my Prince.

DARK LORD: Silence! You listen to me. You spoke out when you were in the synagogue and then he knew who and where you were. That was most unwise.

NIGITH: I couldn't help it. I was compelled to call out to him. He has the power.

DARK LORD: Of course you would speak out in the synagogue, but why did you have to identify him? That only promotes his cause. I have the report before me. You said: "What do we have to do with you, Jesus of Nazareth? You come to destroy us. I know who you are — the — the —

NIGITH: Holy One of God.

DARK LORD: Silence! Silence! You are a religious demon and your assignment was to participate in the religious ceremonies and try to provoke the humans to become entangled in the trappings of the services and forget the meaning of the scripture that was being read and discussed. Wasn't that your assignment? *(PAUSE)* Well, answer me when I speak to you.

NIGITH: You commanded me to be silent, my Prince.

DARK LORD: I know what I told you. I'm telling you now, you worthless slime, answer my questions. You are a religious demon, isn't that correct?

NIGITH: Yes, my Prince.

DARK LORD: What was your assignment?

NIGITH: To disrupt the thinking of the human I was assigned to. To distract and confuse his thoughts.

DARK LORD: You are not the average religious demon, are you?

NIGITH: Oh, no, my Prince. I am a leader of demons. I am the thirty-third rank, my prince. I have had all the training of the secret society of the holy scrolls and can quote any passage from any place in them and coordinate them with any common superstition or craft of human invention.

DARK LORD: I see. Then why did you make such a ridiculous mistake as to call out the title of — of — that one?

NIGITH: I have done my job well for the past twenty years with my human, my Prince. I admit I made a small mistake but I not only have a plan to take back my human but to trap the One sent from God.

DARK LORD: Your "small" mistake revealed your cover and that is why you are back here instead of doing the job that you were trained to do.

NIGITH: I know. I know. But listen to this plan.

DARK LORD: Very well, but it better be worthwhile.

NIGITH: Oh, it is a worthwhile plan, my Prince. I am going to wait for a short season, then I am going back to my human. He is perfect for my purposes. He studies the holy scrolls every day. Then when I take possession of my human again I will take along some of my strongest friends. I will be their leader. Some friends like Oonat, who promotes pride so well, and Atak, who specializes in self-righteousness. The plan is to tell of the Holy One's mighty deeds. Isn't it a marvelous plan?

DARK LORD: This is your plan? This is your marvelous plan? Just kill this — this —

NIGITH: Kill the Holy One of God?

DARK LORD: He is human. He is subject to death. And death is our realm.

NIGITH: But, my Prince, just listen to my plan. It will work.

DARK LORD: Just how will this "plan" of yours work?

NIGITH: My worthy Prince, we will go tell abroad his deeds — and they are great miracles — that many will become so enthralled in his works that they will forget the man himself. He will become insignificant.

DARK LORD: To worship the miracles and not the miracle maker — it just might work. But remember this. If you fail this time you will be sent to the pit and chained there. Do you understand this?

NIGITH: Yes, my Prince. I will not fail. The plan is foolproof.

DARK LORD: Put your plan in effect in a week. That should give you enough time.

NIGITH: *(BOWING OUT BACKWARDS)* Yes, my Prince. Victory to you.

DARK LORD: Yes, victory.

Past/Future

Theme
Only Jesus can free us from our hurtful past.

Summary
Leo, a young man in business, is liked and encouraged by his manager, but he has some hang-ups: his mother and father are still controlling him — so much so that he can't relate to others.

Playing Time	4 minutes
Setting	A business office
Props	Two ropes, computer printout
Costumes	Joel, Leo — business suits
	Momma and Poppa — casual
Time	The present
Cast	JOEL — the manager
	LEO — works for Joel
	MOMMA
	POPPA

JOEL: *(ENTERS ALONG WITH LEO. JOEL CARRIES A COMPUTER PRINTOUT, LEO IS ATTACHED BY ROPES TO MOMMA AND POPPA WHO ALSO ENTER. LEO IS THE ONLY ONE WHO SEES MOMMA AND POPPA)* Now, listen, Leo, I want you to take over this new position and really run with it. I know you'll do a fantastic job.

LEO: Right, Mr. Smith. I'm ready. Thanks again for the opportunity.

JOEL: *(AS HE IS TURNING TO LEAVE)* Oh, Leo, I forgot to tell you that there was a mistake on that last order.

LEO: Oh, I didn't know that.

MOMMA: *(AS MOMMA AND POPPA TALK TO LEO THEY PULL ON THEIR ROPE)* Can't you do anything right, Leonard?

JOEL: Just a mistake. You can correct it easy enough.

POPPA: Look at you. You're a mess. Get yourself cleaned up. How can anybody get so dirty?

JOEL: Can you have the corrected printout on my desk by noon?

LEO: What?

MOMMA: You just think you know everything. Well, you don't know anything, little mister smarty pants.

POPPA: You're just stupid! I knew you couldn't do it right. I knew I couldn't trust you to do anything right. I knew it.

JOEL: I said, can you have the printout corrected and on my desk by noon?

POPPA: You're not listening. Don't you ever listen to your father? Pay attention when I'm talking to you. Pay attention. Get the wax out of your ears and pay attention.

JOEL: Well, Leo?

LEO: Er, uh. What's that, Sir?

MOMMA: You're no good, Leonard. Why aren't you like your brother, William? Now, William is smart. Why can't you be smart, like William?

JOEL: Leo, what is it, the new job? You seem distracted.

POPPA: I don't know what it is with that son of yours. He's just like you. He can't finish a job. He's not going to amount to anything.

MOMMA: He's your son as much as he is mine. Lord knows I never wanted the kid. I wish I'd never had him. He's been trouble from the moment I laid eyes on him.

LEO: No. I'm all right. I'll fix the mistake.

MOMMA: I don't care if it takes you all night. You stay in there until you get that mess cleaned up.

JOEL: Are you sure? I can have Ed do it.

POPPA: That's just like you. Always trying to get out of work. I never saw anyone as lazy as you. Why, if you worked for me I'd fire you. Now get that job done.

LEO: I'll do it. I said I'd do it and I'll do it, all right?

POPPA: Listen, BB brain, I said stick to a job until it's finished. Why, when I was a boy I was working two jobs by the time I was your age. At least you can do one job right.

JOEL: I think it must be the new responsibility, Leo. Now, we all have confidence in you. We all know you can do it. So just relax and I'll have Ed take care of this minor mistake. You just settle into the new work. (*JOEL TAKES THE PRINTOUT FROM LEO*)

MOMMA: You see, I just knew you weren't spending enough time on your homework. Now, you went and did it. You've flunked your test. That's it! No more playing after school. Now, you just get in there and study. No dinner for you tonight. Only smart boys like William get to eat tonight.

POPPA: What is it with you? Are you the greatest loser of all time? Are you ever going to do anything? I doubt it. I really doubt it. Now, you just get out there and mow the lawn and wash the car and then we'll just see how smart you are.

LEO: *(GRABBING THE PRINTOUT BACK FROM JOEL)* No, I'll show you I can do it.

MOMMA: No. Leave it alone. I'd rather do it myself than have you mess it up again and make it worse. Get out from under my feet. Go somewhere — anywhere!

POPPA: Don't I have enough to worry about without having you bothering me all the time? Is your work finished? No, don't ask me for anything. That's all you do is whine for things. Do you think money grows on trees?

MOMMA: What's wrong with Leonard? He doesn't do well in school. He doesn't play sports. He just mopes around the house all day. Can't you do something with him? You ought to understand him, he's just like your side of the family.

POPPA: I sometimes think about what I could have become if I hadn't married you.

MOMMA: You wouldn't have become anything. You were a lazy bum when I married you and you wouldn't have changed.

POPPA: At least I wouldn't be tied down to you and a couple of kids.

MOMMA: Well, you're free to go any time and good riddance.

POPPA: I am going and I don't care if I ever lay eyes on any of you ever again. *(JOEL BEGINS TO EXIT BUT LEO RUSHES TO HIM AND HUGS HIM QUITE INAPPROPRIATELY)*

LEO: No, no, don't leave me. I'll do better. I'll be a good boy. I really will. Just don't leave me. (*JOEL CAN'T BELIEVE WHAT HAS JUST HAPPENED. HE EXITS. LEO BEGINS TO EXIT WITH MOMMA AND POPPA STILL CLINGING TO HIM*)

MOMMA: Leonard, you're just like your father. He was a lazy bum and so are you. You're just lazy. It's your nature. You can't help it. It's just who you are.

POPPA: Listen, idiot! You'll never amount to anything in this world. The world is going to eat you up for breakfast and then throw you up like a piece of garbage.

Moses

Theme

God reaches out to us no matter what our situation — and we have models of that in the Bible.

Summary

A humorous retelling of Moses' encounter with God. Moses is in trouble. He's a shepherd but allergic to sheep and his wife is a nag. In the midst of this turmoil God steps in and talks to him.

Playing Time	3 minutes
Setting	The wilderness of Midian
Props	Staff, sunglasses, baby, lunchbox, fire extinguisher
Costumes	Costume pieces — head coverings, sheep heads
Time	Moses' time
Cast	MOSES
	ZIPPORAH — his wife
	JETHRO — her father
	BUSH
	GOD
	SHEEP

ZIPPORAH: (*ENTERS*) Moses, you've got to get a job. You've been lying around this tent ever since you left Egypt. Don't forget you've got a wife and child to support now.

MOSES: (*AWAKENING*) All right. All right. I'll ask your father if he's got something I can do.

JETHRO: (*ENTERS*) Good morning. How's my new grandson? (*ZIPPORAH NUDGES MOSES*)

MOSES: Oh, yeah, Dad, I've been thinking, is there any little job around the camp you'd like me to do, like counting your gold or something like that?

JETHRO: Looking for a job, huh?

MOSES: No, not really. (*ZIPPORAH NUDGES HIM*) I mean, yes.

JETHRO: Well, I do need a new shepherd.

MOSES: (*SNEEZES*) Sheep? But I'm allergic to sheep!

JETHRO: Well, take it or leave it.

MOSES: I think I'll lea ... (*ZIPPORAH NUDGES HIM*) I mean, I'll take it.

JETHRO: So, go to work. (*JETHRO HANDS MOSES THE STAFF AND EXITS*)

MOSES: (*SNEEZES*) I'll smell like a sheep.

ZIPPORAH: (*PRODUCING A LUNCHBOX*) Get going. I already packed you a lunch. (*SHE EXITS. SHEEP ENTER AND CROWD AROUND MOSES*)

MOSES: (*MOSES PUTS ON SUNGLASSES*) Well, here I am watching these stupid sheep and sneezing my fool head off. (*BUSH ENTERS AND WAVES RED SCARVES FOR FIRE*) Why, look at that bush. It's burning. (*HE RUNS AND GETS FIRE EXTINGUISHER. SHEEP EXIT*)

GOD: (*JUST A VOICE*) Wait a minute. Take off your shoes.

MOSES: Why, what's wrong with my shoes?

GOD: This is holy ground.

MOSES: (*TAKING OFF HIS SHOES*) Who are you?

GOD: I am the Lord your God and I have a job for you.

MOSES: Thanks, Lord, but I already have a job, tending these stupid shee ...

GOD: You will go to Egypt and tell Pharaoh to let my people go.

MOSES: Me?

GOD: Yes, you. Now go. (*BUSH EXITS*)

ZIPPORAH: (*ENTERS*) Moses!

MOSES: Here I am.

ZIPPORAH: Where have you been? I've been looking all over for you. The sheep are scattered all over the mountain.

MOSES: I've been here with this burning bu ...

ZIPPORAH: Yeah? The sun's got to you. What have you really been doing?

MOSES: I can't tell you.

ZIPPORAH: You better tell me.

MOSES: You'll laugh.

ZIPPORAH: No, I won't.

MOSES: Promise you won't laugh?

ZIPPORAH: Of course I won't laugh.

MOSES: Now, you're not going to laugh, are you?

ZIPPORAH: Don't worry. I won't laugh.

MOSES: Okay. I've been talking to God. (*ZIPPORAH SNICK-ERS*) And He told me to go to Egypt. (*ZIPPORAH LAUGHS*) I'm supposed to tell Pharaoh to let the children of Israel go. (*ZIPPORAH GUFFAWS*) Oh, be quiet and pack me a lunch. And you better make it a big one. I'm going to be gone forty years.

Opening Up To Jesus

Theme
Jesus fulfills all our needs.

Summary
At the home of Joash a crowd gathers because Jesus is going there to teach. Joash has his house ready — even a new roof. During the evening friends bring a lame man but can't get to Jesus. What to do? They tear off the roof, of course. Jesus heals the man and the roof gets fixed too.

Playing Time	8 minutes
Setting	The home of Joash
Props	Wine and cups, litter for lame man, pallet
Costumes	Peasants of Jesus' time
Time	The time of Jesus
Cast	JOASH — the master of the house
	SERVANT
	JESUS
	SCRIBE
	ONE PERSON
	ANOTHER PERSON
	FIRST MAN
	SECOND MAN
	HARETH — the lame man
	SOMEONE ELSE

SERVANT: *(ENTERS AND BOWS BEFORE HIS MASTER)* Master, the food is prepared.

79

JOASH: Do you think there is enough?

SERVANT: More than I've ever seen before.

JOASH: I just hope it is enough.

SERVANT: Surely it is. We couldn't have that many people.

JOASH: Where Jesus goes there's always a crowd.

SERVANT: People have started to arrive already.

JOASH: Save the wine until later, when Jesus arrives. And make sure you keep it away from all those scribes. Make sure Jesus gets the first cupful and then you may serve it to the others.

SERVANT: Master, the men who were working on your house said it was finished.

JOASH: The roof? It sure took them long enough. I don't like dealing with someone I don't know. Since Hareth had that accident I haven't had anything around here fixed correctly.

SERVANT: It sounds like Jesus is here and a lot of people came with him.

JOASH: I wonder if there are any scribes.

SERVANT: There are always a few following Jesus.

JOASH: They always make trouble and there's nothing anyone can do. *(JESUS ENTERS WITH A LARGE CROWD FOLLOW-ING)* Welcome, Lord. Will you have some wine?

JESUS: Later, thanks, Joash. These people came to hear my teachings and I must not disappoint them. *(TO CROWD)* Friends, you must turn from evil and turn to God.

ONE PERSON: But how, teacher? How do we turn from evil?

JESUS: You have heard it said, "An eye for an eye and a tooth for a tooth."

SCRIBE: For it is written.

JESUS: Truly, it is written, but I say to you, do not resist violence. If someone slaps you on the cheek, turn the other cheek to him, that he may slap the other also.

ANOTHER PERSON: I don't understand.

SOMEONE ELSE: Just listen. Maybe you will.

JESUS: And if someone is going to sue you and take you to court, and you lose the case and your shirt is taken, let's say, well, then, I say, give him your coat as well.

SCRIBE: This is radical. This will change the structure of our entire law!

JESUS: Now you all know that the Romans ... (*REACTION FROM THE CROWD*) can force us to carry their gear for a mile.

SCRIBE: Now, what's he going to say, carry their horse as well?

JESUS: I say to you, not only carry their gear the one mile but carry it an additional mile, also. Give to those who ask and be generous to those who want to borrow from you. If you are forced to carry the gear one mile and offer to carry it an extra mile, the first mile you will be walking as a slave, but the second mile you will be walking as a friend.

SCRIBE: I can't believe it. This Jesus is turning our laws upside down. It's ridiculous.

SERVANT: *(ENTERS QUICKLY)* Master, come quickly — the roof.

JOASH: Not now. What? The roof? What do you mean?

SERVANT: *(LEADING HIM OFF)* Oh, it's horrible.

JOASH: What is it? What? *(JOASH AND SERVANT EXIT)* Oh, no! Would you look at that mess? How am I ever going to fix that? *(JOASH AND SERVANT ENTER)* How did you let that happen?

SERVANT: I didn't know about it until it was too late. They had already made the hole in the roof.

JOASH: A big hole. I'll never get that fixed. My new roof. It took so long to ... *(FOUR MEN ENTER WITH A PARALYZED MAN ON A PALLET)* ... get it repaired.

FIRST MAN: We're sorry about the roof, Joash.

SECOND MAN: There was no other way. There was such a crowd.

JOASH: But my roof. I would have asked people to make a way for you if you would have asked me.

FIRST MAN: We were in a hurry. We had to get Hareth to Jesus so he could be healed.

JOASH: But, my roof ... Hareth? It's Hareth you've brought?

JESUS: Brothers, I have witnessed your great faith today. *(TO HARETH)* My son, your sins are forgiven.

SCRIBE: He goes too far this time. Why does he talk that way? That is blasphemy. Does he think he is God? Only God can forgive sins.

JESUS: You scribes, why do you question this way in your hearts? Let me ask you a question.

SCRIBE: Sure, go right ahead.

JESUS: Which is easier to say to a paralyzed man: "Your sins are forgiven and forgotten forever" or "Rise, take up your pallet and start walking ..."

SCRIBE: Ridiculous.

JESUS: "... and keep on walking"? But that you may know positively and beyond a doubt that I, the Messiah, have the right, the authority and the power on earth to forgive sins, *(TO HARETH)* I say to you, arise, pick up and carry your pallet and go home. *(HARETH ARISES AT ONCE)*

HARETH: I'm healed! *(JUMPING ABOUT AND TRYING HIS MUSCLES)* After that fall from the roof a year ago, I've been paralyzed. But I'm healed. I'm healed. *(KNEELING AT JESUS' FEET)* Thank you, Master. You've done it. You've healed me.

ONE PERSON: I've never seen anything like this before.

ANOTHER PERSON: Follow Jesus. You'll see a lot more.

SCRIBE: How do we know that wasn't a trick? He's probably a friend of Jesus.

SOMEONE ELSE: If he wasn't before, he certainly is now.

SCRIBE: I've had enough. I'm getting out of this madhouse. *(EXITS)*

SOMEONE ELSE: And now that the scribe's gone we can celebrate. *(ALL PRAISE AND THANK GOD)*

FIRST MAN: Isn't it wonderful? We've seen a mighty miracle this day. A man's been healed.

JOASH: Yes, it's true, a mighty miracle, but at the expense of my roof. How will I ever get it fixed?

JESUS: Don't worry so much, Joash. Isn't a healing more important than a roof?

JOASH: I suppose so, but it's not your roof.

JESUS: (*LAUGHS*) You're right. But I could fix it for you. I am a carpenter.

JOASH: No, I couldn't let you do that.

HARETH: I couldn't either.

JOASH: Hareth, how does it feel to be completely well again?

HARETH: It's like being born all over again.

JOASH: Interesting concept.

HARETH: But it feels much better to know my sins are completely forgiven ... (*HE HUGS JESUS*) ... and completely forgotten. Jesus, I love you.

JESUS: And I love you. Well, Joash, I think I'm ready for that cup of wine now. (*JOASH MOTIONS TO SERVANT WHO SERVES JESUS*)

HARETH: Don't worry, Joash. I'll fix your roof.

JOASH: But you'll need time to gain your strength back.

HARETH: I'm stronger now than I was before my fall. I'll fix your roof.

JOASH: Well, thanks. That's great.

HARETH: It's the least I can do for a man that "opened up" his home to me. *(THEY BOTH LAUGH AND HUG)*

JESUS: You see, Joash, everything can be healed.

U R Fair I C

Theme
Pharisees need to be shocked out of their ridiculous religiosity.

Summary
Fairisee has appointed himself lawmaker, judge, and prosecuting attorney and the accused is Jesus. Scribe is supposed to respond in the usual manner but he upsets the entire procedure by thinking.

Playing Time	3 1/2 minutes
Setting	The home of Fairisee
Props	None
Costumes	Fairisee, scribe — robes appropriate for their station
Time	The time of Jesus
Cast	FAIRISEE — a judge
	SCRIBE
	JESUS

FAIRISEE: *(ENTERS ALONG WITH SCRIBE)* Next case.

SCRIBE: The next case before this high Pharisaic tribunal is the church versus Jesus.

FAIRISEE: Is the accused present?

JESUS: *(RISING)* Yes, your honor.

FAIRISEE: What are the charges?

SCRIBE: The charges are that Jesus of Nazareth and his disciples are not fasting.

FAIRISEE: A weighty charge. Who brings these charges?

SCRIBE: You do.

FAIRISEE: I do? Oh, yes, I do.

SCRIBE: How many times do you fast, just as an example?

FAIRISEE: And an excellent example, too. I fast two times a week, as the law demands.

SCRIBE: What law are you referring to?

FAIRISEE: The excellent Pharisaic law, of course. That's fair.

SCRIBE: I see.

FAIRISEE: Yes, of course. And how many times do you, Jesus, and your disciples fast?

JESUS: Once a year.

FAIRISEE: Once a year?

SCRIBE: Only once a year!

FAIRISEE: Of all the unrighteous nonsense. It can hardly compare with what I do, can it?

SCRIBE: Hardly. Once a year. Ha!

FAIRISEE: That comparison is fair.

SCRIBE: I see.

FAIRISEE: Very fair.

SCRIBE: I see.

FAIRISEE: And by what law do you only fast once a year?

JESUS: The law of Moses. We fast on the Day of Atonement.

SCRIBE: That is the law. For it is written.

FAIRISEE: But we have supplemented the law with extra laws that are added to the law to enhance it and to allow practitioners of these more inclusive laws to draw closer to holiness. That's fair.

SCRIBE: What?

FAIRISEE: What do you mean "what"?

SCRIBE: I mean, uh ...

FAIRISEE: You're not supposed to say, "what." When I say that something is fair you are supposed to respond, "I see."

SCRIBE: I know.

FAIRISEE: Then why did you say, "what"?

SCRIBE: Uh, because I didn't understand what you said. When I say, "I see," it indicates that I understand. In this case I didn't understand, so I said, "what."

FAIRISEE: You don't have to understand. You just have to respond.

SCRIBE: I see.

FAIRISEE: Good.

SCRIBE: I see.

FAIRISEE: That's fair.

SCRIBE: What is?

FAIRISEE: Will you give the proper response?

SCRIBE: Oh, sorry. I guess I was thinking.

FAIRISEE: Well, stop it. Thinking is dangerous and often a waste of time. That's fair.

SCRIBE: Why?

FAIRISEE: Stop talking and start responding.

SCRIBE: I see.

FAIRISEE: Now, that's better. That's the correct response.

SCRIBE: I see.

FAIRISEE: Good. Now, let's get back to the accused. Jesus only fasts once a year by his own admission. I fast twice a week by my own spotless record. Which is more holy?

SCRIBE: I see.

FAIRISEE: Not yet.

SCRIBE: Sorry.

FAIRISEE: Who is more holy?

SCRIBE: Jesus.

FAIRISEE: That's wrong.

SCRIBE: I see.

FAIRISEE: I am most holy. It's quite plain.

SCRIBE: No, it isn't.

FAIRISEE: What are you saying?

SCRIBE: I'm saying it's not plain at all. God gave the law to Moses that states that we must fast but once a year. Why should you add anything to God's law?

FAIRISEE: Because by doing these extra things it makes you more holy.

SCRIBE: Who says?

FAIRISEE: I say.

SCRIBE: And who made you the judge?

FAIRISEE: I did.

SCRIBE: God is our lawgiver. I'd rather He be my judge. That's fair.

FAIRISEE: I see. What am I saying?

JESUS: This happens every time people begin to think about what they're saying and doing.

SCRIBE: That's fair.

FAIRISEE: I see.

Transfigu-what?

Theme

How does the transfiguration of Jesus affect us?

Summary

Peter, James and John discuss the transfiguration.

Playing Time	3 1/2 minutes
Setting	The home of Peter
Props	None
Costumes	Peasants of Jesus' time
Time	The time of Jesus
Cast	PETER — a disciple of Jesus
	JAMES — another disciple
	JOHN — and another one

PETER: *(ENTERS ALONG WITH JAMES AND JOHN)* James, I know what happened but I can't believe it.

JAMES: I know what you mean, Peter.

JOHN: But Jesus commanded us to tell no one what we have seen.

PETER: Okay, I won't tell anyone what I've seen. I'll just talk about what I felt. I was really afraid.

JAMES: Me too. I couldn't get over it. When Jesus' clothes started to shine, I didn't know what to think.

JOHN: I was afraid too, but should we talk about it?

PETER: It's all right. Jesus just meant we shouldn't tell anyone who isn't one of us. How about when Elijah and Moses appeared?

JAMES: I wonder why they showed up? And why Moses and Elijah?

PETER: I don't know. I didn't know what to say. I still don't.

JAMES: Well, it's something we'll never forget.

JOHN: That's right.

JAMES: I'll tell you what, after what Jesus has been talking about lately I'm glad we had something exciting happen.

JOHN: Do you mean his talk about dying?

PETER: Yeah. Can you believe it? Boy, he really gave me the going over for telling him he wouldn't suffer and be killed.

JAMES: Yeah. He called you Satan.

PETER: Don't remind me.

JAMES: I agree with him.

PETER: (*PUNCHES JAMES*) C'mon.

JOHN: Certainly not. You're not as smart as Satan.

PETER: Okay, okay, I don't want to talk about that.

JAMES: I should think not.

PETER: I want to talk about what happened on the mountain.

JOHN: What about the cloud?

JAMES: And the voice. That was the voice of God.

PETER: No kidding.

JOHN: "This is my beloved son, hear him."

JAMES: And then the cloud disappeared.

PETER: And Moses and Elijah disappeared.

JAMES: I don't know what it means but I know I felt great.

JOHN: I guess we needed to feel great about Jesus being the Son of God. I think he's preparing us for something in the future.

JAMES: Yeah.

JOHN: That great feeling seals it for me.

PETER: I know I'll never doubt again. This experience is it for me. I'll never doubt Jesus or anything he says again.

TOGETHER: *(CLAPPING EACH OTHER ON THE BACK)* Yeah!

The Presentation

Theme

The amazing incidents surrounding Jesus' presentation in the Temple predict his future.

Summary

Mary, the mother of Jesus, and Joseph, her husband, reminisce about Jesus as a baby and how it was when they went to the Temple to dedicate him to God.

Playing Time	3 minutes
Setting	The home of Joseph and Mary
Props	None
Costumes	Peasants of Jesus' time
Time	The time of Jesus
Cast	MARY — the mother of Jesus
	JOSEPH — her husband

MARY: *(ENTERS ALONG WITH JOSEPH)* Did you have a good day, dear?

JOSEPH: Yes, Mary, I did. I'm tired.

MARY: Are the boys with you?

JOSEPH: Yes, they're washing for the evening meal.

MARY: Why don't you just relax until they all come in. You've been working too hard.

JOSEPH: We all worked hard. The boys are a big help.

MARY: I know Jesus is.

JOSEPH: He sure is. I don't know what I'd do without him.

MARY: He's growing up so fast. Someday he'll have his own family.

JOSEPH: I know. It's difficult to think of them leaving home.

MARY: I seems like such a short time ago that Jesus was born.

JOSEPH: Yes, it does. Remember when we took him to the Temple?

MARY: Of course I remember. That was a glorious day, when we presented him to the Lord God. Our firstborn.

JOSEPH: What was the old man's name? You know, the one who wanted to hold Jesus.

MARY: What was his name? I should remember. I know I didn't want anyone touching my baby, but you said it was all right.

JOSEPH: Simeon.

MARY: Simeon, that was it. He took Jesus in his arms and prayed a prayer.

JOSEPH: Yes. He prayed to God, saying that Jesus was the salvation prepared by God for His people.

MARY: And the salvation to the Gentiles.

JOSEPH: That's right — a revealing light for the Gentiles.

95

MARY: Then there was that widow — Anna.

JOSEPH: She lived in the Temple. She blessed him too.

MARY: And said that he'd be the redemption of Jerusalem.

JOSEPH: The thing about that day that has always troubled me was what Simeon said about the sword.

MARY: I've often wondered what it meant — that a sword would pierce my soul.

JOSEPH: I know that thinking of Jesus leaving home would be enough to pierce my soul with a sword.

MARY: Mine too.

JOSEPH: Well, then, we must enjoy the time he is with us.

Forced By The Spirit

Theme

Why was Jesus compelled by the Holy Spirit to go into the wilderness to be tempted?

Summary

Sharon has just returned from her vacation and Karen, her friend, wants to hear all about it. But the vacation was a wilderness experience, not what it was supposed to be.

Playing Time	3 minutes
Setting	The workplace
Props	Bible
Costumes	Contemporary, office
Time	Today
Cast	KAREN
	SHARON

KAREN: *(ENTERS ALONG WITH SHARON)* So, did you have a good time on your vacation? We saved a lot of work for you.

SHARON: My vacation was terrible.

KAREN: That bad?

SHARON: It sure was.

KAREN: You went to the perfect vacation spot — the tour brochure said it was "the garden spot. The perfect place for a relaxing vacation."

SHARON: More like a wilderness than a garden.

KAREN: What could have gone wrong? A wilderness?

SHARON: Yes, a wilderness. Let me tell you, enough went wrong to make it difficult.

KAREN: Well, tell me.

SHARON: Listen, maybe I can talk about it sometime, but not now. I'm too close to it. Do you know what I mean?

KAREN: So what do you think went wrong?

SHARON: I don't want to talk about it.

KAREN: I know — later.

SHARON: Yes, later.

KAREN: Maybe the Spirit led you there.

SHARON: What?

KAREN: The Holy Spirit.

SHARON: What are you talking about?

KAREN: Like Jesus. The Holy Spirit led Jesus into the wilderness.

SHARON: Jesus? Where does it say that?

KAREN: In my reading for today. Right here in Mark.

SHARON: Listen, we have to get to work. We'll talk at lunch.

KAREN: All right.

SHARON: But wait: why would the Holy Spirit lead Jesus into the wilderness?

KAREN: I thought we were going to talk about it later.

SHARON: Oh, come on, why would he do that?

KAREN: I don't have any idea. Why would your tour guide lead you into the wilderness?

SHARON: I don't know.

KAREN: It says he was compelled by the Spirit.

SHARON: Compelled? Forced?

KAREN: Wow, that's a little stronger than "led." Wow, "forced."

SHARON: At least I wasn't forced to go on the tour to the wilderness.

KAREN: Were you tempted?

SHARON: Tempted? No, not really. Not any more than usual.

KAREN: Well, Jesus was forced to go into the wilderness where he was tempted by Satan.

SHARON: Why would the Holy Spirit lead Jesus into temptation? The Holy Spirit is our comforter.

KAREN: Well, he did.

SHARON: Yes, but why? Do you think the Holy Spirit leads us into temptation?

KAREN: He might. He forced Jesus to go into the wilderness. If we're followers of Jesus he would probably do the same to us.

SHARON: But why?

KAREN: I don't know. Why did he do that to Jesus?

SHARON: Jesus couldn't sin. He was God. Maybe it was to prove to Satan that he was really God and that he had the power over sin ...

KAREN: And power over Satan.

SHARON: Then, if we're like Jesus, we can have power over sin, too.

KAREN: And through Jesus, power over Satan, too.

SHARON: Right.

KAREN: We'd better get to work. See you later.

SHARON: Right. Later.

KAREN: Later is when I get to hear all about your wilderness experience.

SHARON: I will tell you all about it ...

TOGETHER: Later.

Second Sunday In Lent
Mark 8:31-38

Suffering

Theme
Why do believers suffer?

Summary
Reggie has just received the news that he is dying and he and his wife, Sylvia, struggle with why this should happen to them and where God's comfort is.

Playing Time	5 minutes
Setting	The home of Reggie and Sylvia
Props	Phone
Costumes	Contemporary, casual
Time	The present
Cast	REGGIE
	SYLVIA

REGGIE: *(ENTERS ALONG WITH SYLVIA. REGGIE ON THE PHONE)* Well, that does it, I guess.

SYLVIA: The doctor?

REGGIE: Yeah.

SYLVIA: Does he want more tests?

REGGIE: No more tests.

SYLVIA: What then?

101

REGGIE: He says more tests won't help.

SYLVIA: Oh, no. *(SHE RUNS TO HIM AND THEY EMBRACE)*

REGGIE: It's what I expected.

SYLVIA: But not what we hoped for.

REGGIE: No, not what we hoped for.

SYLVIA: Where's God when you really need Him?

sit

REGGIE: I don't know.

SYLVIA: We're His children. Why won't He help us?

REGGIE: I don't really know.

SYLVIA: We're not immature Christians. We've known the Lord now for 27 years. We've volunteered in the church for most of those years.

REGGIE: Yes, we have.

SYLVIA: Then why won't God heal you?

REGGIE: Maybe we shouldn't ask.

SYLVIA: What do you mean?

REGGIE: I mean, maybe we should leave that in His hands.

SYLVIA: You're just depressed.

REGGIE: No, no, I don't think so.

SYLVIA: Then how can you say we should just leave it in God's hands?

REGGIE: Well, we have to, don't we? I mean, what can we do?

SYLVIA: Do? I guess we've done all we can do.

REGGIE: Well, then?

SYLVIA: I'm not just letting you die. I'm not.

REGGIE: What choice do we have?

SYLVIA: We can try new treatments.

REGGIE: You know we can't do that. There's no more money. There's no more time.

SYLVIA: *(CRYING)* Why? Oh, why? *Stand*

REGGIE: I don't know. *stay seated*

SYLVIA: Why won't God take care of us?

REGGIE: Do you know what I was thinking the other day?

SYLVIA: What?

REGGIE: I was thinking that this was good.

SYLVIA: This is good? What are you saying?

REGGIE: I'm saying that maybe God allows this sort of thing so we can be more like Christ — suffering, you know.

SYLVIA: Oh, that's hogwash and you know it.

REGGIE: No, I don't. Think about it. Job suffered, didn't he?

SYLVIA: Sure, he did.

REGGIE: And the disciples suffered. And Jesus suffered.

SYLVIA: Oh, I don't want to talk about it.

REGGIE: I think we have to think about it. I'm dying.

SYLVIA: Please, don't.

REGGIE: We have to talk about it.

SYLVIA: Why? Why do we have to talk about it?

REGGIE: Because it's something we have to go through together. What else have we been through that we didn't talk about?

SYLVIA: Nothing. We always have talked about everything.

REGGIE: Right. No matter how tough it was. So, this is something we can talk through.

SYLVIA: But I don't want to.

REGGIE: To tell you the truth, I don't want to either.

SYLVIA: Must we?

REGGIE: I think we must.

SYLVIA: All right then.

REGGIE: Everyone dies, sooner or later.

SYLVIA: I know.

REGGIE: So, we just know my death is coming soon, that's all. The doctor said he can ensure that the pain will be minimal.

SYLVIA: What about my pain?

REGGIE: I guess Jesus will have to be your doctor.

SYLVIA: I know he will. I know that. I just don't want to lose you.

REGGIE: This is just another time you'll have to depend on Jesus instead of me.

SYLVIA: I know. You've always been there for me.

REGGIE: No. I let you down plenty of times.

SYLVIA: I can't seem to remember any of those times now.

REGGIE: Well, I remember. Plenty of times.

SYLVIA: I know. But you're forgiven.

REGGIE: I know I am. I can face this with you ... and Jesus.

SYLVIA: Do you think that's why we suffer — to be an example to others?

REGGIE: I don't know. I guess so. Maybe. I know I want to end well. As an example to others. It's important, isn't it — to end well?

SYLVIA: Yes, it's important.

REGGIE: I want to. You can help me. You can help me end well.

SYLVIA: I'll help. I'll be right here beside you.

REGGIE: I know you will. You'll be just like Jesus. Right here beside me.

SYLVIA: Yes, just like Jesus.

REGGIE: And we can offer our suffering to him and ask him to teach us through it.

SYLVIA: Yes, I guess so.

REGGIE: We could.

SYLVIA: Yes, it's important.

REGGIE: Yes. We will. I love you. *(THEY EXIT)*

3/19/06

Third Sunday In Lent
John 2:13-22

Stand Up For Jesus

Theme
Who will speak out for Jesus when it becomes necessary?

Summary
The worship service is interrupted by several people and we're thrust into a drama before we are aware of it. People are complaining about Jesus and how he disrupted things by cleansing the Temple. A Levite and a priest speak out against Jesus and finally someone asks if there isn't someone who will come to Jesus' defense.

Playing Time	3 minutes
Setting	Your church
Props	None
Costumes	Whatever is appropriate for your church
Time	The present
Cast	SMITTY
	WILL — a Levite
	HENRY — a priest
	SALLY

SMITTY: *(ENTERS AND CROSSES TO PODIUM)* I have an announcement that I failed to make at announcement time.

WILL: *(STANDS IN THE CONGREGATION)* May I interrupt?

SMITTY: I just have an announcement. It's about a car in the parking lot.

107

WILL: Please. This is important.

SMITTY: All right. Go ahead.

WILL: I'm shocked about what you people are doing. Shocked. You are actually singing about Jesus.

SMITTY: Just a minute, sir.

WILL: A mistake, that's what it is, a mistake. Do you know him? Do you?

SMITTY: Excuse me, sir, you are creating a disturbance. We must ask you to sit down.

WILL: *(CROSSING TO THE PODIUM)* Do you know who you're singing about? I doubt it.

SMITTY: Sir, if you'll just sit.

WILL: Jesus. That's who you're singing about, isn't it?

SMITTY: I was just trying to make an announcement.

WILL: I can't believe it. You don't even know who it is you're singing about. Let me tell you something. He's not as great as you say. Not at all. He's a bigoted Nazarene — that's what he is.

I'm a Levite, and I know for a fact that this Jesus of Nazareth is a phony. He claims to be the Messiah. He could get killed for that. Let me tell you what he did to me. I lost my job on account of this guy Jesus. He caused me to lose all the money I had tied up in livestock.

I sell animals in the Temple. I mean, I used to sell animals in the Temple. He threw us all out of the courtyard. Every one of us. Most of the others rounded up their cattle and sheep but I sold doves. Well, I couldn't catch birds again, could I?

Believe me, I was angry. Well, that's my story. And you are actually singing songs about him. All I can say is, any man who would cause a lot of people to lose their jobs is not a man to sing about.

HENRY: *(RISING AND CROSSING TO PODIUM)* I can vouch for the authenticity of this man's report, about Jesus of Nazareth.

WILL: Thank you very much.

HENRY: I wanted to bring up another point about him. I too, have been involved with this Jesus, which, I dare say none of you people who sang about him have.

He argued with me many times. I am a priest in the Temple. The very Temple that he said would be destroyed. And not only that, but he also predicted he would restore it again in three days.

Three days, eh? Some of the things he says are strange and would be funny if the problem weren't so serious. The problem is people actually believe him. Crowds follow him everywhere. The people believe he is a prophet. They worship him.

This is the ultimate slap in the face for those of us who are priests. We are the ones who must protect the purity of worship. We just can't let any crowd-pleaser mouth a few words of so-called wisdom and quote a few scriptures and then expect people to worship him. And you are the only people who can stop it. We priests can't do it alone. We can't do it all. You people have to help.

You people have to wake up and take a stand against this man Jesus. You've heard what this man has told you about losing his life savings. And you heard my plea for purity of worship. We both ask you to take care in what you are doing and watch who you're singing about.

SALLY: *(RISING AND CROSSING TO PODIUM)* May I say something? I'm a little confused, as I'm sure many of my friends are. I just feel we should defend our Lord, somehow. Now, I'm not a Bible scholar and I can't quote the scriptures ... I don't know. I just feel someone should say something.

SMITTY: I agree. You people, won't you say something? Can't someone defend Jesus? Isn't there anyone here who will stand up for Jesus? *(THE HOPE IS THAT SOMEONE FROM THE AUDIENCE WILL SAY SOMETHING IN FAVOR OF JESUS, BUT IF NOT THE ACTORS EXIT.)*

3/26/06

Fourth Sunday In Lent
Ephesians 2:4-10

In The Heavenly Places

Theme

It is best to have all the answers about how to enter heaven before you need them.

Summary

It's never stated in the Bible that entrance into heaven is easy. Two candidates lining up at the pearly gates express two opposing views, one quite worldly and the other simply trusting in Jesus. But who is this third person helping the worldly-wise person? He seems to have all the answers. Are the answers any good?

Playing Time	5 1/2 minutes
Setting	Just this side of Heaven's pearly gates
Props	None
Costumes	Street clothes except for Jesus, who wears a robe
Time	The present
Cast	BOOT — a confident candidate for heaven
	WILY — an unsure candidate
	DICK — he's got all the answers
	JESUS

BOOT: (*WILY ENTERS FOLLOWED BY DICK AND BOOT. DICK IS GUIDING WILY TO A PLACE WHERE JESUS WILL ENTER. BOOT IS MARCHING, COUNTING CADENCE*) I don't know, but I've been told, the streets up there are paved with gold. Sound off. One, two. Sound off. Three, four.

WILY: Oh, no. Not another one of those.

DICK: Don't pay any attention to him.

BOOT: Sound off. One, two. Sound off. Three, four.

WILY: They drive me crazy.

DICK: Try not to think about him. Concentrate.

BOOT: I don't know but it must be so, everybody wants to go.

WILY: He makes me nervous.

DICK: Forget him.

WILY: Okay, okay. But it's really difficult with that going on in my ear.

DICK: Remember what I told you.

WILY: I sure hope I do remember.

BOOT: Sound off. One, two. Sound off. Three, four.

DICK: All right, what if He (*MOTIONING TOWARD THE GATE*) asks you about your life?

WILY: I've got the answer for that, all right. I'll just say I've led a good life. That's an easy one.

DICK: That's pretty good. You studied the manual, didn't you?

WILY: I studied a lot. But I'm not so good at remembering things.

DICK: Well, that's okay. I'm right here to help you out when you get in a jam. I've got all the answers.

BOOT: Sound off. One, two, three, four. One, two, THREE, FOUR.

WILY: I'm telling you, that guy makes me nervous.

DICK: You have no reason to be nervous.

WILY: That's easy for you to say. Of course I'm nervous. Anyone would be nervous. I've got to say just the right thing so God will let me into heaven. You bet I'm nervous. I'm real nervous.

DICK: Calm down. You've got the answers. Be confident. This is no big deal. Don't ever let God see you sweat.

WILY: Are you nuts? This is a big deal, the biggest deal. I want to make sure I get in.

BOOT: I don't know but I've heard it said, to get up here you gotta be dead.

WILY: (*TO BOOT*) Stop it! (*TO DICK*) Make him stop it!

BOOT: What's wrong?

WILY: Your singing. It makes me nervous.

BOOT: Nervous, about what?

WILY: About getting into heaven, of course. Aren't you nervous?

BOOT: Not really.

WILY: It really makes me nervous when people talk about death.

BOOT: Why?

WILY: Why? Just because death is spooky. That's why.

BOOT: And why is death spooky?

WILY: It just is and everyone knows it and if you don't you're weird.

BOOT: Well, I'm sorry if I made you nervous. I won't march anymore. I just get excited when I think about heaven and being with Jesus and all the saints and whatever we'll be doing there. Doesn't that excite you?

WILY: I'm just worried about getting in.

DICK: I told you not to worry. (*TO BOOT*) And you, BUTT OUT!

BOOT: Sorry.

DICK: There, now, that seems to have taken care of that.

WILY: I'm still nervous.

DICK: Okay, a little refresher: What if He (*MOTIONING TO-WARD THE GATE*) asks you why He should let you into His heaven?

WILY: I'll just say, "Because I've become a better person than I used to be. I've climbed the ladder of spiritual holiness, learning to be better every day."

DICK: Very good. You see, you don't have a thing to worry about.

WILY: I do feel better.

DICK: Good. Now, remember the scales?

WILY: Yes, yes, the scales. Let me see. Ah, yes, I remember. I could answer that I have done a lot of good things in my life and when God weighs those things on a scale that they will far out-weigh the bad things in my life.

DICK: (*PROMPTING WILY*) And that you have lots of friends ...

WILY: Oh, yes. And I have lots of friends praying for me to get into heaven.

DICK: Good. Good.

WILY: Here comes someone.

BOOT: It's Jesus.

WILY: How do you know?

BOOT: I just know. It's Jesus, all right.

DICK: It's Jesus, all right.

JESUS: (*ENTERS AND CROSSES TO OTHERS*) Two more people wanting to get into heaven.

BOOT: Yes, Lord.

WILY: Are you Jesus?

JESUS: I am.

WILY: I'm ready for any question you might ask me.

JESUS: I'm sorry, but you can't enter heaven.

WILY: I searched for God in my own way but I searched with all my heart.

JESUS: You were deceived. I am the way, the truth, and the life. No one comes to the Father except through me. (*TO BOOT*) You are welcome, my son.

WILY: (*TO BOOT*) Why are you allowed to enter heaven?

BOOT: Well, I trust Jesus. I believe in him.

JESUS: And he has for a long time. Welcome, son. (*JESUS HUGS BOOT*)

WILY: But Jesus, please, I want to enter heaven with all my heart. Please, have a heart.

JESUS: No.

WILY: But I was brought here by this angel of light. I thought that was supposed to happen to me when I died.

JESUS: It does look like an angel of light, doesn't it.

DICK: I am an angel of light.

WILY: There, you see.

JESUS: Only to those who want to see you that way. Get out of here now, and take your victim with you.

WILY: (*AS SHE IS BEING LED AWAY BY DICK*) Oh, no. I trusted you and you tricked me. O-o-o-h, n-o-o!

DICK: Right. It's still working.

WILY: But why? Why did you take me to heaven if you knew I couldn't get in? Why?

DICK: (*LEADING WILY OFF TO HER FATE*) It's the first and the best torment.

BOOT: (*AS HE CROSSES TO JESUS, SINGING*) I don't know but as I roam, this here place sure feels like home. Sound off, one, two. (*BOOT AND JESUS CROSS TOWARD HEAVEN*)

God's Voice

Theme

How do we distinguish God's voice from all the clutter we hear every day? There are a few who will hear.

Summary

A crowd is gathered to hear Jesus teach. But what a crowd. Among the believers are the pragmatists, the skeptics, and the non-believers.

Playing Time	4 minutes
Setting	Holy Land
Props	Wheat grain, flowerpot with soil
Costumes	Period costume for Jesus, modern for crowd
Time	The time of Jesus
Cast	JESUS
	SOMAN — a face in the crowd
	BUNO — another face in the same crowd
	GARNA — a doubting face
	NAMAS — the last face
	GOD'S VOICE

(SOMAN, NAMAS, GARNA AND BUNO ENTER.)

SOMAN: Well, here we are.

NAMAS: Jesus will be here soon.

GARNA: What if he doesn't show up?

SOMAN: We'll have wasted a whole day. We could have been buying and selling.

BUNO: I don't have a lot of time to waste here, you know.

GARNA: I'll bet he doesn't show.

NAMAS: He'll be here. And it'll be worthwhile. What he has to say is always so inspiring.

BUNO: Here he comes now. *(JESUS ENTERS, CARRYING A FLOWERPOT)*

SOMAN: What's that he's carrying?

BUNO: Looks like a flowerpot to me.

GARNA: What? A flowerpot? What's he have that for?

NAMAS: It'll be a good teaching, I'll bet.

JESUS: The time has come for the Son of Man to be glorified and exalted. I want you to understand this. *(HOLDING UP GRAIN OF WHEAT)* Do you see this grain of wheat? It's not going to produce more wheat as it is, is it? The only possible way it can do that is to be planted. *(PLANTING GRAIN OF WHEAT IN THE SOIL IN THE POT)* When it's planted in the earth it dies, right? And then and only then can it grow and then we could have a lot of wheat from this one little seed.

Anyone who loves his life, as it is, will lose it; and the person who despises his life as it is in this world can exchange that life for eternal glory. If anyone wants to serve me, he must continue to follow me; for my servants must be where I am. If a person follows me, the Father will honor that person. Now my soul is troubled and distressed; and what shall I say — Father, save me from this time of trial and agony? That is the very reason I came here. Rather, I will say, Father, glorify and honor your own name.

GOD: I have already done this and I will do it again.

(*JESUS EXITS*)

SOMAN: (*LOOKING AT THE SKY*) Do you think it's gonna rain?

BUNO: Did you hear that thunder? Sounds like a gully-washer for sure.

GARNA: What are you two talking about?

SOMAN: Didn't you hear that thunder?

GARNA: You're kidding, right?

BUNO: No. There was a loud clap of thunder.

GARNA: Well, I didn't hear it.

SOMAN: Well, there was thunder. And that means it's gonna rain.

BUNO: Thunder means a storm. That's for sure.

GARNA: You two are crazy. That's for sure.

SOMAN: Now, tell the truth, didn't you hear anything?

GARNA: I didn't hear any thunder.

NAMAS: (*SUPER-SPIRITUALIZING*) I heard something, but I think it was an angel that spoke to him.

BUNO: A what?

NAMAS: An angel. I'd swear it was an angel.

GARNA: You're crazier than they are.

SOMAN: An angel, eh? That's a good one. An angel.

GARNA: I didn't hear anything.

BUNO: We know. You told us.

SOMAN: There are no such things as angels. Where do you people get that stuff?

NAMAS: There are so angels. I saw one once.

SOMAN: You probably see a lot of things, don't you?

NAMAS: No, not a lot.

BUNO: But you see things.

GARNA: I didn't see anything. And I didn't hear any ...

BUNO: You didn't hear anything. We know.

SOMAN: Well, since you heard an angel, what did the angel say?

NAMAS: I couldn't hear what he said. I just heard something.

BUNO: What a waste of time.

NAMAS: No. It's not a waste of time.

BUNO: What did Jesus say?

SOMAN: I don't remember. (*EXITS*)

BUNO: I heard thunder. It's going to rain. It's going to rain and I won't get my work done. I've wasted a whole day out here. (*EXITS*)

121

NAMAS: You must have heard it.

GARNA: Did you really hear something?

NAMAS: Yes, yes, I did.

GARNA: Well, I didn't.

NAMAS: I did. It was beautiful. An angel. I heard an angel.

GARNA: Well, I missed the thunder. I missed the angel. But what did Jesus say? I missed that too.

NAMAS: I don't remember, exactly. But I heard an angel. (*THEY EXIT*)

H/23

Jesus' Visit

Theme

How do we help a brother or sister who is having trouble with their belief? It's difficult but the people who knew Jesus had the same problem. We can learn from them.

Summary

Carl is having trouble believing in Jesus and Christianity. He relates to Thomas, the disciple, and witnesses Thomas' encounter with the risen Christ.

Playing Time	3 1/2 minutes
Setting	Modern day — anywhere
Props	None
Costumes	Period costume for Jesus, Peter, and Thomas
	Modern for Carl and Nance
Cast	CARL — a Christian who has some doubts
	NANCE — his friend
	JESUS
	THOMAS — a disciple
	PETER — his friend

CARL: (*ENTERS ALONG WITH NANCE*) I just can't.

NANCE: Well, of course not.

CARL: But I want to live like a Christian.

NANCE: I know you do.

CARL: I just can't.

NANCE: It's difficult but not impossible.

CARL: I want to be strong. I fail so miserably.

NANCE: Sometimes. Not all the time.

CARL: I know, but I want to be more like Jesus.

NANCE: Well, that's what the Holy Spirit is doing in your life.

CARL: But, I have doubts.

NANCE: I do too, sometimes.

CARL: I know I'm a Christian, but, you know what? What if the whole thing is just fiction?

NANCE: Christianity, you mean?

CARL: Yes, what if it was all made up by the apostles and early Christians?

NANCE: That would be a lot of material to make up.

CARL: I know, but let's say it was possible.

NANCE: Okay. Let's say it was possible to write the entire Bible as a work of fiction. What about those disciples? They saw Jesus after he was dead and came back to life. That wasn't fiction.

CARL: I know they saw him. But what about Thomas?

NANCE: He had some doubts. Just like you.

CARL: That's me, I guess. I'm just like Thomas. We have to live this Christian life without seeing Jesus. All on faith. That's tough to do. I could believe as strongly as the disciples if I could touch Jesus.

NANCE: You really mean that. What about faith?

CARL: Faith? I need some right now.

(THE SCENE SWITCHES TO PETER AND THOMAS AS NANCE AND CARL WATCH)

PETER: We have seen the Lord! He was here with us.

THOMAS: Unless I see in his hands the marks made by the nails, and put my fingers into them and place my hand into his side, where the spear was thrust, I will never believe that he is alive.

JESUS: *(ENTERS)* Thomas, reach out your finger here and touch my hands and place your hand in my side. Don't be faithless any longer. Believe!

THOMAS: *(FALLING DOWN AND WORSHIPING)* My Lord and my God!

JESUS: You believe me because you have seen me. Blessed and happy and to be envied are those people who haven't seen me and have trusted me anyway.

NANCE: You're just like Thomas. That's you.

CARL: No, that's not me.

NANCE: What do you mean? You just saw it. You said you were just like Thomas.

CARL: I just saw it but I still don't believe it.

NANCE: What kind of proof do you want?

CARL: I don't know.

JESUS: How about this. Why don't you come and put your finger here and touch my hands and place your hand in my side. You don't have to be faithless any more. You can choose to believe! (*CARL CROSSES TO JESUS AND TRIES BUT CAN'T PUT HIS FINGER ON JESUS' HANDS*) What's wrong? I thought that's what you wanted to do.

CARL: I did. But now I can't do it.

JESUS: Why not?

CARL: I don't need to. (*WORSHIPING*) My Lord and my God!

JESUS: How's your faith now?

CARL: Not as shaky as it was.

JESUS: Good. Keep working at it.

CARL: I will.

Third Sunday Of Easter
Luke 24:36b-48

The Cure For The Slump

Theme
If we could talk to Jesus, how would that change us?

Summary
Dale is in a spiritual slump and James is trying his best to help him but can't seem to budge him.

Playing Time   3 minutes
Setting   A neutral playing area
Props   Handcuffs
Costumes   Contemporary, casual
Time   The present
Cast   DALE — in a slump
        JAMES — his friend
        POLICE DETECTIVE 1
        POLICE DETECTIVE 2

JAMES: (*ENTERS ALONG WITH DALE*) D'you know what?

DALE: What?

JAMES: I didn't understand tonight's teaching. Did you?

DALE: What?

JAMES: Weren't you listening?

DALE: To you or the teaching?

JAMES: Either one.

DALE: Neither one.

JAMES: What's wrong with you?

DALE: I don't know. I can't seem to put my finger on it. I'm in a slump, I guess.

JAMES: A slump?

DALE: Yes, I guess so. I don't know.

JAMES: What's wrong?

DALE: I just said I don't know.

JAMES: Well, what about tonight's teaching?

DALE: I got lost in it, I guess.

JAMES: To tell you the truth, I guess I did too. I guess I just can't appreciate the entire situation. Jesus' disciples were just talking about him and he appears.

DALE: It does seem a bit unbelievable.

JAMES: And the two who were on the road to Emmaus had just seen Jesus and were relating that experience to the others who hadn't seen him.

DALE: Well, that's it, isn't it? That's the entire teaching.

JAMES: Yes, that's about it. I didn't get much out of it.

DALE: You know I didn't.

JAMES: Maybe we're both in a slump.

DALE: Are Christians allowed to get in a slump?

JAMES: Christians do get in slumps?

DALE: Yes, I guess we're human.

JAMES: I wonder how you get out of the slump.

DALE: I don't know. I'm too much in a slump to care.

(*DETECTIVE 1 AND DETECTIVE 2 ENTER*)

DETECTIVE 1: All right. All right. What's going on here?

JAMES: Who are you?

DETECTIVE 2: We'll ask the questions here.

DETECTIVE 1: Now, what were you doing the night of April 26? (*SUPPLY THE ACTUAL DATE YOU PERFORM THIS VIGNETTE*)

DALE: I don't know.

JAMES: I can't remember.

DETECTIVE 1: You should remember.

DETECTIVE 2: Yeah, you should. That's today's date.

JAMES: Oh, yeah, it is.

DETECTIVE 1: You gettin' smart with us?

DALE: No, not at all.

DETECTIVE 2: They need to get smart, eh, Packy?

DETECTIVE 1: Yeah, that's right. You two need to get smart and start answering some questions.

DETECTIVE 2: Yeah, so where were you tonight?

JAMES: We just came from the Bible study.

DETECTIVE 1: Which you slept through, right?

JAMES: No, no. Not at all.

DALE: We heard every word.

JAMES: Yes, we did. We were just discussing it.

DETECTIVE 2: You were, eh?

DALE: Sure.

JAMES: Yes, we sure were.

DETECTIVE 1: You were also discussing how you are both in a slump, isn't that right?

JAMES: Well ...

DETECTIVE 2: Answer the question.

DALE: Well, I guess we did say something along that line.

DETECTIVE 1: Did you or did you not say you were in a slump?

JAMES: Are we being arrested?

DETECTIVE 2: No, we just want a little information.

DALE: I want to call my lawyer.

JAMES: I am your lawyer.

DETECTIVE 1: You're a lawyer and you're in a slump?

JAMES: That's about it. I hate to admit it, but it's true.

DETECTIVE 2: You ought to be ashamed of yourself.

JAMES: I am. I really am.

DETECTIVE 2: Do we take them in?

DETECTIVE 1: I guess so. It looks like they're guilty.

DETECTIVE 2: As guilty as you get.

DETECTIVE 1: Cuff 'em. I don't want any trouble with these two. (*DETECTIVE 2 PUTS HANDCUFFS ON DALE AND JAMES*)

DALE: I didn't commit any crime!

DETECTIVE 2: Yeah, yeah. That's what they all say.

DETECTIVE 1: Being in a slump IS a crime. And you're both going to pay for it. All right, take them away.

JAMES: (*BREAKING DOWN*) Listen to me. Listen to me. All right. I did it. I was in a slump. I admit it. But it wasn't my fault. It was all his fault. He made me do it. He's the one. He was in a slump and he dragged me into it. I swear, it wasn't my fault. I just fell in with the wrong crowd. You've got to believe me. It wasn't my fault.

DETECTIVE 1: You make me sick. Get them out of here.

DALE: I'll get you for this. You're not going to get away with this. I'll get you, I swear I will. I'll get you. You're going to pay for this. You'll see. I'll get you if it's the last thing I do.

DETECTIVE 2: I'll tell you. They sing a different song when they're caught, don't they?

DETECTIVE 1: They sure do. Boy, oh boy, being in a slump just does not pay.

DALE: I'm sorry. I didn't mean to do it. I didn't mean it. I didn't.

JAMES: I'm a lawyer. I know your case won't stand up in court because you didn't read us our rights.

DETECTIVE 1: You don't have any rights.

JAMES: Of course we have rights. You're law officers. You should know that.

DETECTIVE 2: Well, that's where you're wrong. We're not law officers, we're church police.

DALE: Church police. Oh no!

DETECTIVE 1: (*PUSHING THEM OFF*) I'll tell you, it's good to get this vermin off the street.

The Shepherd, The Wolf, And The Sheep

Theme

The Good Shepherd, Jesus, will look after you if you know him.

Summary

It's bedtime for the three lambs and they want a story. The storyteller tells the story of "The Three Little Lambs." It's an exciting story in which the three lambs take part. The Wolf attacks but is killed by the Shepherd. It all ends well.

Playing Time	6 minutes
Setting	A pasture
Props	None
Costumes	Sheep costumes, a wolf costume, a Jesus robe
Time	Bedtime — story time
Cast	STORYTELLER — Jesus
	LAMBY — a sheep
	FLEECY — a sheep
	WOOLY — a sheep
	WOLFEN — a wolf

STORYTELLER: (*ENTERS WITH LAMBY, FLEECY, AND WOOLY FOLLOWING*) Come along now. It's time for bed.

LAMBY: Will you tell us a bedtime story?

FLEECY: Please tell us a bedtime story.

STORYTELLER: All right. All right. I'll tell you a story. Which one?

WOOLY: Tell us about "The Three Little Sheep."

FLEECY: Yes, yes, "The Three Little Sheep."

LAMBY: Yes, please tell us that one.

STORYTELLER: (*FEIGNING IGNORANCE*) I don't know that one.

FLEECY: Yes, you do.

LAMBY: Sure, you know it.

WOOLY: Tell us. Tell us.

FLEECY: "The Three Little Sheep." Tell us. Tell us.

LAMBY: Please. Please. Please.

STORYTELLER: I don't remember. How does it go?

LAMBY: You remember.

WOOLY: Tell us. Tell us.

FLEECY: Once upon a time ...

STORYTELLER: Once upon a time ...

LAMBY: There were three little sheep ...

STORYTELLER: Oh, I do remember now. Let's see, what were their names?

WOOLY: "Wooly."

FLEECY: "Fleecy."

LAMBY: And "Lamby."

STORYTELLER: That's right. (*LOVINGLY TOUCHING THE HEAD OF EACH ONE AS HE SAYS THEIR NAMES*) Wooly, Fleecy, and Lamby. And they were good little lambs. (*THE SHEEP ACT OUT WHAT STORYTELLER TELLS*) Every day the shepherd would lead them to a pasture full of juicy grass and watch them as they filled their little sheep tummys.

But one day as Wooly, Fleecy, and Lamby were eating the juicy grass, they wandered far from the other sheep and it was getting late in the day and they all began to feel afraid.

FLEECY: What will we do?

LAMBY: I think we're lost.

WOOLY: I'm afraid.

STORYTELLER: ... they said. They began to cry softly because they thought the mean old wolf would sneak up on them and eat them. They huddled together for comfort.

LAMBY: I'm not very comforted.

STORYTELLER: ... said Lamby.

WOOLY: Just because we're together like this won't help if the mean old wolf comes.

STORYTELLER: ... Wooly whined.

FLEECY: I wish our master was here.

135

STORYTELLER: ... Fleecy added with a whimper. (*FLEECY WHIMPERS*) And then, they all heard something in the forest. Something big was making a lot of noise and coming through the underbrush.

LAMBY: Oh, no! It's the wolf!

STORYTELLER: ... Lamby said, huddling closer to the other two.

WOOLY: I'm getting out of here.

STORYTELLER: ... screamed Wooly, as he broke into a wobbly trot.

FLEECY: Wait, wait for us.

STORYTELLER: ... yelled Fleecy, as he and Lamby followed Wooly as fast as their little lamb legs could carry them. (*WOLFEN ENTERS, GROWLS, AND CHASES THE LAMBS*)
And indeed it was the wolf, and he was running after them. As they glanced back they knew he was gaining on them. They knew that he soon would catch them and eat them.

WOLFEN: Aha, I will soon catch you and eat you!

STORYTELLER: The wolf was a blur of black and gray matted fur and his ghastly red tongue was licking his slobbering lips.

LAMBY: C'mon! Run! Run!

STORYTELLER: ... Lamby yelled.

WOOLY: I can't run any faster.

STORYTELLER: ... screamed Wooly.

FLEECY: Oh, no!

STORYTELLER: And then, when the wolf was about to reach out and grab Fleecy, Fleecy twisted his ankle in a hole and fell.

FLEECY: Oh, no!

STORYTELLER: ... screamed Fleecy. The wolf could taste leg of lamb.

WOLFEN: Mmmm. Leg of lamb! (*WOLFEN GRABS FLEECY*)

STORYTELLER: Lamby heard Fleecy's screams and stopped.

LAMBY: It's Fleecy! The wolf has Fleecy!

STORYTELLER: ... screamed Lamby.

LAMBY: We have to help Fleecy!

STORYTELLER: But the wolf already had Fleecy and was dragging the frightened lamb back to his lair.

LAMBY: It's no use.

STORYTELLER: ... cried Lamby.

LAMBY: We could never get Fleecy away from the wolf. We'd just get caught ourselves.

WOOLY: But we have to try.

STORYTELLER: ... said Wooly.

WOOLY: We have to. He's our brother.

STORYTELLER: So, Wooly and Lamby ran back to where the wolf had caught Fleecy. There was blood on the ground but no wolf and no Fleecy.

LAMBY: Fleecy's gone.

STORYTELLER: ... cried Lamby.

LAMBY: We'll never see him again.

STORYTELLER: And Wooly and Lamby held each other and cried. (*LAMBY AND WOOLY CRY*) And cried. And cried some more. For they had lost their brother. And that's the end of the story. A very sad ...

WOOLY: No! No!

LAMBY: That's not the way the story ends.

STORYTELLER: It's not?

LAMBY: No. Remember? The shepherd comes to help.

WOOLY: Yes, yes, the good shepherd.

STORYTELLER: And who is the good shepherd?

WOOLY AND LAMBY: You are!

STORYTELLER: I am?

LAMBY: Yes. You come ...

WOOLY: ... and rescue Fleecy.

STORYTELLER: Oh, yes. I seem to remember now.

WOOLY: So, Wooly and Lamby ran back to where the wolf had caught Fleecy.

STORYTELLER: So, Wooly and Lamby ran back to where the wolf had caught Fleecy. There was blood on the ground but no wolf and no Fleecy. And Wooly and Lamby held each other and cried. (*LAMBY AND WOOLY CRY*) And cried. And cried some more. For they had lost their brother. And then the shepherd came.

LAMBY: The good shepherd.

STORYTELLER: And then the good shepherd came and comforted Lamby and Wooly, and said, "I am the good shepherd; and I know my sheep, and you know me, don't you?"

LAMBY AND WOOLY: We know you. You're the good shepherd.

STORYTELLER: And the good shepherd followed the tracks of the wolf and came upon him while he was in his lair. He was about to eat Fleecy. And the good shepherd killed the mean wolf and rescued Fleecy.

WOOLY: Yea!

LAMBY: Yea!

FLEECY: Really, really yea!

STORYTELLER: And so Fleecy was hugged a lot and loved a lot because he was back with his brothers and the mean old wolf was dead.

LAMBY AND WOLLY AND FLEECY: Yea! Yea!

STORYTELLER: And now you've had your story. Now it's time for bed.

WOOLY AND LAMBY AND FLEECY: All right.

STORYTELLER: So, what did you learn from the story?

LAMBY: I don't know.

WOOLY: Uh, I don't know either.

FLEECY: I don't know. Maybe I ought to run faster.

STORYTELLER: Well, maybe you aren't supposed to learn any-thing. After all, you're just lambs. Just be lambs and enjoy the story.

LAMBY AND WOOLY AND FLEECY: And know your shep-herd.

STORYTELLER: Yes, and know your shepherd.

LAMBY AND WOOLY AND FLEECY: The good shepherd.

STORYTELLER: Yes, and know the good shepherd.

The Orphan

Theme

Talking to someone about love, even the love of God, is a poor substitute for loving that person.

Summary

Dale is an orphan and is feeling the pangs of not having a loving parent. Wyn tries to help, but it turns out to be just talk. Wyn has no ability to love Dale, and Dale is left feeling worse.

Playing Time	3 minutes
Setting	Your church
Props	None
Costumes	Whatever is appropriate for your church
Time	The present
Cast	DALE — the orphan
	WYN — Dale's companion

WYN: *(ENTERS WITH DALE)* Want to go have some ice cream?

DALE: Yeah, I guess so. Why not?

WYN: Well, what did you think of the Bible study?

DALE: It was all right, I guess.

WYN: Jesus has a lot of love to give to us, doesn't he? Today's lesson made that clear.

DALE: To tell you the truth, I don't feel loved.

WYN: That's important to you, isn't it?

DALE: Important to me? You bet it is. Isn't it important to you?

WYN: Why, of course it is. Being loved is probably the most important need of everyone in this entire world.

DALE: Then why are you giving me a hard time?

WYN: I'm not. I just wonder why you mentioned the fact that you didn't feel loved.

DALE: Because I've been having a difficult time with the Bible teaching lately. I know that God loves me, but I don't feel loved.

WYN: Was there ever a time that you felt loved?

DALE: Well, I guess so. I don't know. I guess so.

WYN: When?

DALE: When did I feel loved?

WYN: You want to feel loved, right?

DALE: Right, I do.

WYN: Well, I just wanted to know if you ever felt loved before.

DALE: I can't remember.

WYN: I was just thinking — if you've never felt love before, how would you know the feeling if you felt it?

DALE: I don't really know. I guess I would just know, that's all. How does a baby know it's loved?

WYN: If a baby is well taken care of and has a lot of touching, I suppose the baby would feel loved.

DALE: Yeah, I guess so.

WYN: Were you ever taken care of like that?

DALE: I'm an orphan.

WYN: An orphan. I didn't know that.

DALE: My mother and father were both killed in a plane crash. I was a month old.

WYN: Who raised you?

DALE: I was raised by foster parents and then when I was twelve I was put in an orphanage.

WYN: Were you adopted?

DALE: I was too old. No one wants an older child.

WYN: And you can't remember feeling loved?

DALE: No. Never.

WYN: Did you ever have a good friend?

DALE: A good friend — no.

WYN: How about Jesus?

DALE: I know what you're thinking — Jesus is my friend; he died for me. Right?

WYN: Well, that was quite friendly, wasn't it?

DALE: Now that you mention it, it was.

WYN: Well?

DALE: I told you this need that I have because I thought you wouldn't give me a bunch of spiritual mumbo-jumbo.

WYN: I didn't mean it to sound like spiritual mumbo-jumbo. I just wanted to establish who Jesus is in your life.

DALE: Jesus is my friend, I guess. I pray and talk to him daily but I still don't feel loved. I still want that warm, cozy feeling.

WYN: Do you know what? I think I understand what you mean. You know with your mind that you are loved, but that isn't enough for you. You want to feel it too.

DALE: I really want to have someone to love me like Jesus loves me.

WYN: Would that do it?

DALE: I think it would.

WYN: You need a friend. Did you ever try being a friend to anyone?

DALE: I guess I've heard that one before: "If you want a friend, be a friend." That still doesn't make the lonely feeling go away.

WYN: I was thinking a little deeper than that.

DALE: Like someone you could share your innermost secrets with, like I just did with you.

WYN: Sure.

DALE: And someone I could go have ice cream with, like we're doing.

WYN: Right. Do you know what? I know what I'll do.

DALE: What's that?

WYN: I'll pray for you. (*WYN EXITS, LEAVING DALE STANDING ALONE*)

Sixth Sunday Of Easter
John 15:9-17

Father — Son

Theme
Marriage to a non-Christian — what are the problems? The main problem is love and being unequally yoked.

Summary
Scott is serious about Lonnie and they want to get married, but Lonnie is not a Christian. Scott's dad talks to him about the problem of love, a very necessary ingredient in a marriage.

Playing Time	3 minutes
Setting	Scott's home
Props	Newspaper
Costumes	Contemporary, casual
Time	The present
Cast	SCOTT — is in love
	DAD — Scott's Dad

SCOTT: (*ENTERS. DAD IS READING THE PAPER*) Hiya, Dad. How was your day?

DAD: Not bad. Nothing much out of the ordinary. How about you?

SCOTT: Oh boy, it was some day.

DAD: Well, it must have been. Something happen at track practice?

SCOTT: No. Track practice was a dream.

DAD: A dream. That's hard to believe.

SCOTT: A dream. Everything's a dream.

DAD: Are you okay?

SCOTT: Sure, Dad. I'm great.

DAD: You're talking funny.

SCOTT: Am I?

DAD: And you're acting funny. Now what is it?

SCOTT: Well, I'm in love.

DAD: Oh, no. Not again. Found a new girl, eh? Puppy love?

SCOTT: Woof, woof. No. This is real love this time.

DAD: The real thing, eh?

SCOTT: It's Lonnie, Dad. We really do love each other.

DAD: It's true love this time.

SCOTT: Yes, it is. It really is true love. And I know what you're going to say: "You're too young. You can't support a wife yet."

DAD: No, I wasn't going to say either of those things. But you said — "wife."

SCOTT: I sure did. Lonnie and I have decided to get married. We've worked it all out, Dad. She has a great job at the telephone company and I'll finish my last year at school and then I'm sure to find a good job.

DAD: It sounds like you have worked it all out. That's good. What I was going to ask was if you had prayed about it.

SCOTT: Whoa now, Dad, that's not fair. You know Lonnie isn't a Christian.

DAD: I wasn't trying to be unfair. I'm sorry if it sounded that way. I guess I was just wondering if Lonnie had come around to the way you believe, that's all.

SCOTT: Dad, listen. I love Lonnie and she loves me. The religion part of it will have to be worked out.

DAD: Scott, don't you know it has to be "worked out" before marriage? What if it doesn't get "worked out" at all — ever?

SCOTT: Trust me, Dad. Lonnie loves me. She'll come around. You'll see. The first thing is we have a lot of plans to make for the wedding.

DAD: Scott ...

SCOTT: Dad, wait. Don't quote scripture to me. I know it as well as you do. I know what you were going to say. "Don't be unequally yoked." Right?

DAD: I wasn't going to quote scripture because I know you know it as well as I do. But since you mentioned it, how about First John 4:7...?

SCOTT: ... and 8. I remember that. We used to sing it. (*SINGING*) "Beloved, let us love one another ..."

DAD: Whoa! That's enough.

SCOTT: You don't like my singing.

DAD: You're ready for a record contract.

SCOTT: (*SINGING*) "Beloved, let us love one another ..." Well, Lonnie and I love each other.

DAD: Of course you do. But it isn't the same kind of love.

SCOTT: Sure it is. I love her. She loves me. Love is love.

DAD: No. All love is not the same. You're a Christian.

SCOTT: I know. And Lonnie is not. We can handle that.

DAD: It's not something you have to handle like making out a budget. This is much more important than anything else you'll ever do together.

SCOTT: I know it's important, Dad.

DAD: Yes, I think you do, but I don't think you know that it's the most important thing that you can do for the success of your marriage.

SCOTT: *The* most important thing?

DAD: Yes, it is. As a Christian you have the Holy Spirit living in you and therefore you have a self-sacrificing love to give to Lonnie. And you have a love in you that can forgive anything she will ever do.

SCOTT: I do, and Lonnie has that kind of love for me.

DAD: Not if she's not a Christian, she doesn't.

SCOTT: She has forgiven me several times.

DAD: Now wait a minute, Scott. Don't you see? Lonnie doesn't have the love of God available to her so she cannot respond with that greater love that only God provides. She cannot return the love that you give her. She cannot forgive completely and she will never have her love need fulfilled.

SCOTT: In other words, you're saying that the Christian's love is better. Can't a person just work on it and get better at it?

DAD: Not really. God's love isn't our love increased to a greater degree. It's a Godly love and therefore a person can't attain it for herself. It's a characteristic of God that shines through us. God's love cannot shine through those who aren't submitted to God.

SCOTT: So, our love would be lopsided.

DAD: It really would. She would expect you to meet the love need in her life that only Jesus can fulfill. It would be frustrating for you and for her because she would be unfulfilled.

SCOTT: And you're saying I couldn't fulfill her love needs.

DAD: That's one thing that I'm saying. Only God can really love each one of us as we need to be loved — unconditionally. We humans botch it up. We love selfishly sometimes.

SCOTT: I guess that's true.

DAD: Well, what do you think?

SCOTT: I think Lonnie and I have some more talking to do together.

DAD: Let's pray together first.

SCOTT: And then I could just tell Lonnie what you told me. Do you think she might understand?

DAD: She says she loves you. She just might understand. It's a place to start.

SCOTT: I'll do it. Thanks, Dad.

DAD: Sure. (*SCOTT EXITS*)

Search For The Treasure

Theme
There is an ancient treasure that wise people have longed for — communication with God. Jesus made that available to all people. The word of God is truth. The truth will last for all time. That is a treasure when people find it.

Summary
Two archeologists are digging for treasure in the ruins of an ancient city. They find a rock that tells of a time when God and man communicated.

Playing Time	5 minutes
Setting	The site of an ancient city
Props	Archeologist's tools, map, stone tablet
Costumes	Sturdy hiking gear
Time	The future
Cast	AILY — an archeologist
	BEA — Aily's companion

AILY: (*ENTERS ALONG WITH BEA, LOOKING AT MAP*) This is the mountain.

BEA: I don't know.

AILY: I'm sure of it.

BEA: We're standing on an entire range of mountains. All of these mountains look alike to me.

AILY: But this one shows the scars of an ancient city, many times ravaged and many times rebuilt.

BEA: But is it the right city?

AILY: That, we will have to discern by what we can find here.

BEA: A lot of stones.

AILY: But stones shaped by hand.

BEA: Still a lot of stones.

AILY: Enough stones to build a city. The prophecy stated: "Evenly spaced twixt the salt and tide, mounts the treasure of the bride."

BEA: And you say this is the mountain that's evenly spaced between salt and ...

AILY: "Salt" could mean the lake of salt that lies due east, the one we discovered two days ago.

BEA: Then the "tide" is the ocean to the west.

AILY: Yes. Probably. The ocean would have been much closer then than it is today.

BEA: That would make this mountain equally distant between the two.

AILY: This is the only city ruin of the size we're looking for in this area that fits the ancient prophecy.

BEA: And then we can find the "treasure of the bride."

AILY: Yes. The "treasure of the bride." What do you suppose it is?

BEA: A treasure. It must be worth the search.

AILY: Many have searched before us and failed.

BEA: But we have the map. Do you really think it's accurate?

AILY: The shepherd boy that sold it to me had no idea what he had. It is of the correct vintage. We're the first expedition to have this map.

BEA: Unlimited treasure. What do you think it is?

AILY: We only know it is something that people have searched for for ages.

BEA: (*PICKING UP A STONE TABLET*) Look here. This might be something. (*HANDING IT TO AILY*) What does it say?

AILY: This has been inscribed. It's an important declaration of some kind. I can just make out the inscription, or at least some of it. Some of the markings are faded. "Pledge — something — city — something — something — put on a garment — something — height power."

BEA: "Pledge — city — put on a garment — height power." What language is it written in?

AILY: A very ancient language. Let's see. From the arrangement of the words this could be the ancient word "to sit."

BEA: "Sit down in the city"?

AILY: Hmm, "sit." What do you do when you sit?

BEA: It could be lots of things. I sit when I'm tired.

AILY: A person sits and makes judgments.

BEA: Sit and wait. People do that a lot.

AILY: That could be it. "Sit and wait for the height power." It probably means wait in the city. Maybe this city.

BEA: Maybe. "Height power." Something powerful. Maybe it's the treasure. Whoever controlled a treasure would have power.

AILY: Could be. Let's see. "Something — height power." This is really hard to read. "Height power." Hmm. The words are arranged so that this could be a preposition. In that case it would be "power in the heights" or "power from a height." It's a small word. Maybe "out of." "Power out of a height."

BEA: So, what do we have? "Sit and wait for a power out of a height."

AILY: That might be it. Now this part — "Pledge."

BEA: Read the entire thing again.

AILY: What have we got here? "Pledge — something — sit and wait in the city — something — put on a garment — power out of a height."

BEA: What is this word?

AILY: Well, with its position in the phrase it could modify the word "pledge."

BEA: Then it could be a type of pledge.

AILY: Now that I look at it, I don't think so. It could be the ancient words for the "Pledge of the Father."

BEA: "Pledge of the Father"?

155

AILY: An ancient phrase meaning the inheritance.

BEA: "The pledge of the Father — sit and wait in the city — something — put on a garment — power out of a height." Is that it?

AILY: That's all I can decipher.

BEA: What's it mean?

AILY: It might mean we're on the right track. If the power is derived from the treasure that so many people have searched for, all we need to do is sit and wait.

BEA: Sit and wait! That doesn't make any sense. We didn't travel all the way to this God-forsaken land to sit and wait.

AILY: What did you say?

BEA: I said, why should we stop searching now when we think we've found the ancient city and maybe the treasure. We'd be crazy to stop now.

AILY: We're not going to stop searching. But you said, "God-forsaken."

BEA: Well, just look at it. It is God-forsaken.

AILY: It looks that way, doesn't it? But maybe it just looks that way. Maybe we are the God-forsaken ones.

BEA: What do you mean?

AILY: Listen to this: What if the "height power" is power from God? That would be power out of height, wouldn't it?

BEA: God? An almighty being? No one believes in God any-more. That ancient belief is as old as the tablet.

AILY: Exactly. As old as this tablet. Exactly. The "pledge of the Father." "The inheritance of the Father." Don't you see? The inheritance of God is the power from the height.

BEA: But there is no God. We learned that in school.

AILY: Of course we did. We learned what we were taught. Just because it was carefully taught and we cleverly learned it doesn't make it true, does it?

BEA: Well, no. I guess not.

AILY: As scientists haven't we learned that facts are not facts until we can prove them?

BEA: Yes, right. We have discarded many theories. We have discovered many facts.

AILY: Right. The ancients might have found out about truth. Maybe it has been buried along with the artifacts.

BEA: So how would we sit and wait for this treasure so that we can put on the garment of the power out of the height?

AILY: There must be something we can do. No! Nothing. The garment is put on us. That's what the tablet says.

BEA: Sitting and waiting doesn't seem like something two scientists should be doing.

AILY: How about praying?

BEA: What's that?

AILY: Praying is an ancient concept whereby the people of the earth can communicate with God.

BEA: It seems so archaic.

AILY: It is, but look at it this way — if there is a God wouldn't he want to communicate with humans?

BEA: Why would he?

AILY: So he could give them the power. The ancient pledge.

BEA: The treasure!

AILY: The treasure for which people have been searching for ages.

BEA: That has to be it. Power is a treasure. Why would God want to share his power with humans?

AILY: I don't know. Maybe for them to do his work.

BEA: Why would God need someone to do his work for him if he is all-powerful?

AILY: He wouldn't really, but he might want to share it with them so that they could share in his joy in whatever he does.

BEA: It's beginning to make sense. Let's try this praying. Do you know how?

AILY: I've translated some ancient prayers. We'll try it and see what happens.

BEA: Communicating with God could be refreshing. I'm frankly getting bored with humans who think they have all the answers.

AILY: Well, as we're digging we can pray.

BEA: That way we just might "dig up" some treasure.

AILY: "Out of the height."

The Remote

Theme

"Show us the Father." The world is waiting for someone to show them.

Summary

Susan is getting ready to watch television after a hard day's work. She is interrupted by a strange person who invites her to think instead of just accept all the world hands her.

Playing Time	9 minutes
Setting	Susan's television room
Props	Susan — a small remote
	Fly — a large remote
Costumes	Susan — contemporary, casual
	Fly — fright wig, tutu, tennis shoes
Cast	SUSAN — a normal average person
	FLY— an industrial-strength entity
	11 voices on the television
	(Georgina, Wilhimina, Francine, Nona, Gina, Tommie, Alice, Ann, Debby, Winnie, Macie)

(SUSAN IS CLICKING A REMOTE. AS SHE DOES SO PEOPLE SAY THEIR PIECE AS IF THEY WERE ON DIFFERENT CHANNELS ON THE TELEVISION)

GEORGINA: (*A COMMERCIAL*) And when my husband came home and saw how clean the toilet bowl was ...

WILHIMINA: (*A GERMAN COOK*) Now, vee haf to haf a nice plump shicken for ziss soup.

FRANCINE: (*A TALK SHOW*) And I've written several books on that subject. Women just have to make a more positive vibration in the stratosphere.

NONA: (*AN EXCERCISE SHOW*) Tuck it in. Four more. Looking good. Two more. That's it. Rest now. Shake it out.

GINA: (*A SOAP OPERA*) Why is it, David, that every time we kiss, your significant other is lurking nearby?

TOMMIE: (*A WOMAN SELLING*) And for the next hour I am going to slash the price on this solid gold necklace and earrings signed by Mickey Mouse.

ALICE: (*A WESTERN MOVIE*) Be careful out there, Montana, I've had a hankerin' fer ye fer quite a spell.

ANN: (*AN INFOMERCIAL*) You can make as much money as I did and do it in a month with no initial outlay. I retired when I was 27.

DEBBY: (*A HOME IMPROVEMENT SHOW*) Now we attach the particle board to the two-by-fours and then we have to raise the entire wall into place.

WINNIE: (*A MYSTERY*) Mr. Smead was found dead in the library and all the windows and doors were locked. How do you explain that?

MACIE: (*THE NEWS*) Another major earthquake last night rocked the little country of Ubique in Northern Africa.

SUSAN: Well, what will I watch tonight?

FLY: (*ENTERS, FLITTING ACROSS IN FRONT OF SUSAN. FLY HAS A BIGGER REMOTE THAN SUSAN AND SHUTS OFF SUSAN'S REMOTE*) Straighten up, there. I'm your entertainment for tonight.

SUSAN: What the...? Where did you come from?

FLY: (*FLITTING AROUND*) You don't need to know. Just enjoy me.

SUSAN: Enjoy you? I was trying to relax with the T.V. after a hard day.

FLY: Of course, I forgot. Your brain ...

SUSAN: My brain!

FLY: (*SINGING*) You left your brain in Sam Clam's Disco.

SUSAN: What happened to my quiet evening at home?

FLY: Aren't you blessed. You have me instead. Ta-da!

SUSAN: Will you get out of my house!

FLY: I'll leave when my assignment is completed.

SUSAN: Do you mean you're supposed to be here?

FLY: I've been assigned to you.

SUSAN: Whatever for?

FLY: To help you through this difficult time in your life.

SUSAN: What difficult time in my life? I was just trying to relax and watch a little T.V.

FLY: That's it! That's the difficult time in your life.

SUSAN: What, relaxing?

FLY: No, T.V.!

SUSAN: T.V.?

FLY: (*USING THE REMOTE, FLY CHANGES HERSELF EVERY TIME SHE SAYS SOMETHING*) Exactamo! Television — the bug-eyed monster — the baby-sitter — the vast wasteland — the cabinet of flickering images — the hypnotizer — the mesmerizer — the magic box — the canned entertainer — the visual valium — the boob tube. Yes, the T.V., the home of talk shows and wok shows and cartoons and bar tunes and late movies and weight groovies and opera and news and views and retail sales and retold tales and lusts and busts and guns and buns. Yes, the T. and the V. in its entiritee!

SUSAN: You're wearing me out.

FLY: Don't touch that dial. Our show will be right back after these messages. The content of this program in no way reflects the views of the station. Any similarity to persons real or imaginary is purely coincidental. This offer void where prohibited. The decision of the judges is final. Call us at 4 WORLD VIEW, that's the number 4 then the words WORLD VIEW, or visit our web page at www dot worldview dot com.

SUSAN: Just go away. You're getting on my nerves. I just want to be alone.

FLY: But don't you get it? You're not alone. When you're watching television you're inviting a host of people into your home and their thoughts into your mind. Some of these people have good intentions and some are out to harm you.

162

SUSAN: Really? I never thought of that.

FLY: C'mon, think with me. This could be a life-changing experience for you.

SUSAN: I don't need any more life-changing experiences. I just moved here and I have a new job. That's enough for me. I just want to relax.

FLY: I know, "and watch a little T.V."

SUSAN: What's wrong with that? I work hard. (*PAUSE*) Hey, wait a minute, I do work hard. You just happened to catch me at a time that I wanted to relax. Why don't you leave me alone. I'm tired.

FLY: I'm just starting on you. Now listen, did you ever learn anything? I mean really learn anything?

SUSAN: I attended the best schools.

FLY: Don't give me the indignant "I graduated from such and such and what-its-doodle school." I don't have time for it. I've got a job to do and you just need to be quiet and watch and listen, Okay? Okay? Is that all right with you? Huh? Huh?

SUSAN: I got good grades in school.

FLY: We're not connecting here. I asked you if you ever really learned anything and you tell me you got good grades. There's a difference, you know.

SUSAN: I had the best teachers.

FLY: Great! But did you ever question anything they told you? (*PAUSE*) Just as I thought. You never did, did you? Didn't you ever wonder if what those teachers were teaching was the truth?

163

SUSAN: Wasn't it? I mean, it was in the books, wasn't it?

FLY: Whoa! Reality check. How do you know that what was in the books was truth?

SUSAN: I never thought about it.

FLY: And because you chose not to think about it or much else, you have been misguided and many times deceived.

SUSAN: Is that my fault?

FLY: Oh boy, major overhaul here. Well, what do you think? When you go to the restaurant what do you eat?

SUSAN: My favorite foods.

FLY: What kind of clothes do you wear?

SUSAN: What I like and what looks good on me.

FLY: All right, now. Stay with me on this. What do you put into your mind?

SUSAN: Well, I never thought about it much.

FLY: You choose what goes into your mind, don't you? Just like choosing food or clothes. Right?

SUSAN: I guess so.

FLY: You guess so. You don't have any opinions of your own, do you?

SUSAN: I most certainly do. I have opinions. Well, I do. I do.

FLY: You do not.

SUSAN: I DO SO!

FLY: Listen. Just yelling louder and longer than the other person doesn't make it true. Boy, oh boy, have I got a lot of work to do on you. Why do I always get the jellyheads?

SUSAN: Jellyhead!

FLY: Good. I guess your hearing is all right. Yes, jellyhead. You're a jellyhead — tasty and beautiful but empty calories.

SUSAN: You don't see me prancing around in a funny dress and tennis shoes.

FLY: Oh, ho! You're one of those individuals who judge the character of a person by what that person is wearing? A person is not just what you see. A person is certainly more than that. The soul and spirit of a person is the real individual.

SUSAN: Of course, I know that.

FLY: If you do know that, as you say, and you do not practice it, as you also have shown, then you are not only a jellyhead but maybe empty-headed. Listen, if you do not agree with good, sound reasoning, then you must be inconsistent in your own reasoning, which is a definition of being empty-headed.

SUSAN: You're wearing me out.

FLY: Ah, yes. That is because you do not have an opinion of your own. Your opinions are all shallow and are not based on logic, just emotion.

SUSAN: Why don't you leave me alone.

FLY: Because there might just be hope for you. Now maybe I can get to work on you.

SUSAN: What are you going to do to me?

FLY: Change you if I can. I know. I know. The job will take a while, but you weren't doing anything except watching T.V. anyway. (*PAUSE*) Well, you're being quiet. That's a start.

SUSAN: Shocked would be a better word.

FLY: I'll settle for shocked. Now, listen, you need to make some changes in your life.

SUSAN: Like what? I don't much like change.

FLY: Let's get back to the search for truth, shall we?

SUSAN: How would I know the truth?

FLY: Well, you are making progress! You're asking the right questions. How do you know the truth? There are several ways. First, you know the truth by proving it.

SUSAN: Proving it?

FLY: Yes.

SUSAN: Do you mean I have to test everything I hear?

FLY: BINGO!

SUSAN: How do I do that?

FLY: By performing a test on the material presented to you.

SUSAN: Do you have any idea all the stuff I have to look at in a day?

FLY: Now you're beginning to think. You're right, it will be a lot of material and you can't test all of it, but it is important to investigate that which affects your pocketbook or your belief system.

SUSAN: My belief system?

FLY: Oh, I forgot — major overhaul. Yes, your belief system. All people have one.

SUSAN: I don't.

FLY: Sure you do. If you say you don't believe in anything, that's a belief system. A pretty shaky belief system, but it is one nonetheless.

SUSAN: I believe in something.

FLY: Oh, important discovery! What is it?

SUSAN: Well, I, ah, believe in, ah, myself, I guess.

FLY: (*LIKE AN ALARM GOING OFF*) Beep — Beep — Beep. Red Alert. Red Alert. Arm photon torpedoes. Fire on my command.

SUSAN: What did I say? I believe in myself? What's wrong with that? Don't most people believe in themselves?

FLY: Of course they do, but we just said not all people are truthful. Some people are out to harm you. Those harmful people believe that they are right in what they believe and some of them want you to believe as they do.

SUSAN: All right. I'm with you.

FLY: Hooray! Let's get back to your question.

SUSAN: I forgot where we were.

FLY: I know. A short attention span. You had asked me how to know truth.

SUSAN: Oh, right.

FLY: For instance, someone tells you the sun rises every morning in the east. How do you know if what they're saying is the truth?

SUSAN: I could test it.

FLY: Good. Very good. And how would you do that?

SUSAN: I'd get up before sunrise and watch it.

FLY: Great. And if the sun came up in the east?

SUSAN: I'd know the truth, wouldn't I?

FLY: Yes, you would. For one day, at least.

SUSAN: Oh, I get it. I'd have to make the test a lot of times, wouldn't I?

FLY: Right. How many times, do you think?

SUSAN: I don't know. A lot.

FLY: Right. A lot. There is another way. You could trust a person to tell you the truth.

SUSAN: But I can't trust people to always tell me the truth. We already said that. How do I know who is telling me the truth and who isn't?

FLY: Think about it.

SUSAN: Well, whoever it would be would have to be a completely honest person all the time, because if he wasn't he would sometimes be selfish and want to tell me a lie.

FLY: Hey, you ARE thinking!

SUSAN: And this person would have to know everything. I mean everything.

FLY: Why?

SUSAN: Because he would have to know what was good and what was bad and know about everything that had ever been done or would be done because then he would know how to tell what was true and what was a lie.

FLY: Sounds real good. Go on.

SUSAN: And this person ... oh, what's the use. I could never find a person like that.

FLY: Don't give up. You were just on the verge of something.

SUSAN: I was?

FLY: Sure. Now, let's think. Who could know everything and be loving and unselfish?

SUSAN: Well, it sounds like a fantasy — magic.

FLY: A special person, right?

SUSAN: Very special — a perfect person.

FLY: Who would be perfect?

SUSAN: It would have to be ... but I don't believe ... in that.

169

FLY: Maybe it's time to change your belief system.

SUSAN: Well ... what about God?

FLY: God? Who mentioned God?

SUSAN: No one — hey, I did!

FLY: Do you believe in God?

SUSAN: Not really. Well, maybe. There must be truth somewhere. There has to be.

FLY: It would be nice, wouldn't it?

SUSAN: But, God? Who believes in God anymore?

FLY: You'd be surprised. Keep searching. You've made some great leaps forward. Don't stop now. (*FLY PREPARES TO EXIT*)

SUSAN: Wait, where are you going? I need you.

FLY: You don't need me. You can think on your own now.

SUSAN: Hey, I can, can't I?

FLY: (*EXITING*) You sure can. Keep thinking. It's a good idea.

SUSAN: It is a good idea — thinking. Hmm. Now, I wonder how I could find out more about God?

The Remote Revisited

Theme

"Unless a person is born again he cannot see the kingdom of God." Being born again is the beginning of kingdom work.

Summary

Susan is exercizing and is interrupted by Fly, who has returned to help her further become a mature Christian. But she tells him she doesn't need help — she has God to help her.

Playing Time	9 minutes
Setting	Susan's television room
Props	Fly — a hand-held computer, dress, wig, shoes, rings, earrings, necklace, hand-held microphone, apron, cooking spoon, baking mitt, baby doll, rifle, helmet, music score
Costumes	Susan — contemporary, casual
	Fly — fright wig, tutu, tennis shoes
Cast	SUSAN — a normal, average person
	FLY — an industrial-strength entity

SUSAN: (*EXERCISING*) Tuck it in. Four more. Looking good. Two more. That's it. Rest now. Shake it out.

FLY: (*ENTERS, FLITTING ACROSS IN FRONT OF SUSAN. FLY DOES SOME EXERCISES ALONG WITH SUSAN, LEADING HER A LA RICHARD SIMMONS, SINGING ALONG WITH AN OLDIE*) C'mon, Baby, light my fire. Kick it, Baby, kick it higher ...

SUSAN: Oh, no. Hey, you're interrupting my life again.

FLY: (*FLITTING AROUND*) I'm sure it's a welcome interruption. I'm here to help.

SUSAN: I don't need your help anymore. I have my life straightened out.

FLY: Not according to my report. (*PRODUCING A LONG PRINT-OUT. READING*) Naper, Susan, 1200 N. Tingo Trail. Is that address correct?

SUSAN: Yes, yes, it is, but, you don't have to bother with me now. I feel good.

FLY: (*SINGING A LA JAMES BROWN*) You feel good. Knew that you would ...

SUSAN: What happened to my quiet evening at home?

FLY: Aren't you blessed. You have me instead. (*LIKE ZORRO*) I will rescue you!

SUSAN: Rescue me from what? Will you get out of my house!

FLY: You know by now I'll leave when my assignment is completed.

SUSAN: Do you mean I'm your assignment again?

FLY: Who else? (*HUMPHREY BOGART*) Here's looking at you, Babe.

SUSAN: Whatever for? I'm all right now. I gave my life to Jesus!

FLY: I know. It's all here in my report. But you still need help. And I was so successful the last time that I was sent back to help you.

SUSAN: I don't need help now. I'm a confident woman. Or at least I'm in the process.

FLY: That's it! That's where you need help — in the process. And I can help. Look what I helped created the last time I was here. (*LIKE BORIS KARLOFF*) I was working in my lab late one night when my eyes beheld an eerie sight ...

SUSAN: What, is this the top ten hits of the '50s?

FLY: '60s my dear. '60s. Ah, yes, no historical accuracy. (*CHECKING READOUT*) Yes, it's all here. Oh, boy, we need a lot of work here.

SUSAN: Now cut that out. I know who I am and I don't need your help.

FLY: Oh, posh and tush, of course you need my help. Just by saying you don't need my help means you need it all the more. We all need each other. We are in this thing together.

SUSAN: That may be true for the normal human being, but no one has determined what you are. You are certainly not normal.

FLY: Me, not normal? When you cut me do I not bleed? Ouch! The thought sickens me. Of course I'm normal. (*PUNCHES COMPUTER*) Hmmm. Thinks she is only person who is normal. Very interesting case.

SUSAN: I've forgiven everyone who wronged me and forgiven myself and received forgiveness from God.

FLY: Great, greater, greatest! Fantastic foundation, but are you maturing in the faith?

SUSAN: I think so. I meet with some friends and we study the Bible.

FLY: Coffee and tea and the B-I-B-L-E. Now you're talking.

SUSAN: We're really opening up to each other and Jesus is healing all of us through prayer. I accept myself as I am. I love myself. You're wasting your time and certainly my time.

FLY: Listen, I'm on assignment here. I don't waste time.

SUSAN: I have confidence in myself now, and my confidence begins in my heart. And my heart is Jesus' territory. You can see I've changed. Just look at me.

FLY: (*JOHNNY MATHIS*) "Look at me." This is great-a-mundo. This is fantasmigoro. You had a life-changing experience, didn't you?

SUSAN: Why, yes, I have. That's what I've been trying to tell you.

FLY: Hey, little sister, dot dot dash, dash dot dot, I'm getting the message.

SUSAN: Good. So, bye-bye.

FLY: Watch out there. Don't hurt yourself. This Christian stuff is new to you. This is uncharted territory. "Sail ho. Two points off the starboard bow. Man the mizzen. All hands aloft." Hey, I have a question for you. You say you accept yourself. How about your appearance? How about that?

SUSAN: Well, I don't like everything about my physical appearance.

FLY: I thought so. What you need is a complete makeover. (*A HAIR STYLIST*) First we'll take some of this off. A short bob will do it, I think. Just sit down and put your trust in me completely. Your face is much too thin. We need to tease the hair a bit, I think.

(*TEASING*) Ya-da, ya-da, ya-da. Yes, that should do it. (*PLOPS ON A WIG*)

And, of course, that tired old outfit has to go. A new light frilly frock to go along with your new personality. (*PRODUCES A DRESS*) Here, put this on. Good. Good. It looks to me like there's a new you somewhere in there. Some new shoes. Yes, great. Some more rings, earrings, a necklace. Wonderful-a-mous. Jolly-jolly-jump-up.

Now, look at you. You're ready for a Christian talk show. (*HANDING HER A HAND-HELD MICROPHONE*) And now, with her latest Christian rock hit, here's Susan, singing, "If Jesus Could See Me Now Would He Ask Me To Dance?"

SUSAN: Wait a minute. Wait just a minute. It's more important who I am than how I look.

FLY: Whoa and hold your horses! Someone who can think for herself. "Hi ho, Silver."

SUSAN: I'm developing my inner resources.

FLY: Inner resources. Wow-o-wowee, you are a humdinger. You have made progress. "One small step for mankind." Don't you know that how you look on the outside reflects who you are inside?

SUSAN: Wait, that's not all the story.

FLY: "And now you're going to hear the rest of the story."

SUSAN: Well, sometimes I feel like dressing up and sometimes I don't.

FLY: True, true, but you also represent the king of the universe now and the people that you meet will be judging Christianity by what they see when they meet you.

SUSAN: Well, that's probably true.

FLY: But, wait, there's more. You want to be every inch a woman, don't you? You need this, Suzy Homemaker. (*PUTTING AN APRON ON HER, A SPOON IN HER HAND, AND AN OVEN MITT ON HER OTHER HAND WITH A BABY DOLL*) You want to be all you can be in the kitchen, too, don't you?

SUSAN: Yeah, but ...

FLY: Are you a leader? You need to be a leader.

SUSAN: A leader, me?

FLY: Yes, you. (*PRODUCING A HELMET, GUN*) Now, wear this uniform proudly. Salute! March. (*MARCHING AROUND WHISTLING SOUSA'S "STARS AND STRIPES FOREVER"*) Ta-ta, ta-ta-ta, ta-ta-ta.

SUSAN: This is being a leader?

FLY: Of course. Now, you're ready for any battle. "Now listen, let's Simonize our watches. All right. Here's the plan. You take the right flank and I'll take the left flank and we'll each have a baked potato with our steaks and the *soup du jour* of the day."

SUSAN: This gun is a little heavy.

FLY: Of course it's a little heavy. So's life. So's the battle. But you have to be prepared for the battle. The battle for truth, the battle for right, the battle for the mind, the battle against ring around the collar.

SUSAN: I think I have battle fatigue.

FLY: Do you know you have a lovely voice, my dear? You should be in the choir. (*HANDING HER A MUSIC SCORE*) Sing along with this one. (*SINGING*) "When You're Doing The Washin' Of Life, Jesus, Don't Hang Me Out To Dry."

SUSAN: Now wait a minute.

FLY: What for? We're on a roll here.

SUSAN: No, we're not on a roll. I'm not doing this. This isn't right.

FLY: Maybe you're right. This gun should be over this other shoulder.

SUSAN: No! I'm not wearing this stupid stuff.

FLY: Stupid stuff? Hey, I brought this all the way from ... well, never mind where I brought it from. I brought it just for you to make you the complete Christian woman.

SUSAN: (*TAKING STUFF OFF*) I am a complete Christian woman. I have Jesus. Or rather he has me and that makes me complete. How much more complete can I be? I don't need this stuff to be who I am.

FLY: Oh, yes, you do. (*PUTTING SOME THINGS BACK ON HER*)

SUSAN: Oh, no, I don't. (*TAKING IT BACK OFF*)

FLY: Yes, you do. (*PUTTING SOME THINGS BACK ON HER*)

SUSAN: No, I don't. (*TAKING IT BACK OFF*)

FLY: You do. (*PUTTING SOME THINGS BACK ON HER*)

SUSAN: I don't. (*TAKING IT BACK OFF*)

FLY: Do. (*PUTTING SOME THINGS BACK ON HER*)

SUSAN: Don't. (*TAKING IT BACK OFF*)

FLY: D. (*PUTTING SOME THINGS BACK ON HER*)

SUSAN: D. (*TAKING IT BACK OFF*)

FLY: (*PUTTING SOME THINGS BACK ON HER*)

SUSAN: (*TAKING IT BACK OFF*)

FLY: (*PUTTING SOME THINGS BACK ON HER*)

SUSAN: (*TAKING IT BACK OFF*) STOP IT! WILL YOU KEEP YOUR HANDS TO YOURSELF!

FLY: I'm just trying to make you into a mature Christian woman.

SUSAN: Well, you can't. Only God can do that. I'm not going to become a mature Christian woman by carrying all this stuff around with me.

FLY: You could build up your muscles.

SUSAN: I don't want big muscles. No one is going to make me into anything. I'm letting Jesus remake my life into what he intended it to be.

FLY: There might be hope for you.

SUSAN: What do you mean?

FLY: Hope. Hope. You know what that means, don't you? It springs eternal.

SUSAN: Of course there's hope for me. God the Father loves me and so does Jesus, so much so that he died in my place and the Holy Spirit comforts me at all times — even now when you are trying to make me so uncomfortable.

FLY: Hey, you're getting pretty spunky.

SUSAN: Listen to me. Here's the scoop from the group.

FLY: Now you're talking my language, little sister.

SUSAN: I said listen!

FLY: Right.

SUSAN: I don't need your crazy interference with my life. I like my life just the way it is. Is that coming in loud and clear? Is that perfectly plain to you?

FLY: All right, Susan. Go for it.

SUSAN: I am sick and tired of people telling me what I'm supposed to be. I'm not a "Total woman" or a "Liberated woman" or an "Emancipated woman" or a "Sensual woman" or a "Prosperous woman" or a "Little woman" or a "Dominating woman" or a "Motivated woman" or an "Assertive woman" or a "Dress-for-success woman" or a "Good Housekeeping woman" or a "Vanity Fair woman." I'm just me. Just me! Do you hear me? Just me. Me. Susan. M-E. Me!

FLY: I think you're trying to tell me you're happy with who you are.

SUSAN: Exactomundo.

FLY: Great. I think that's just great.

SUSAN: Good-bye. And don't honor me with another one of your visits, all right?

FLY: My, aren't we a little touchy. You see how I'm appreciated.

SUSAN: I'm sure you won't feel so bad since you're leaving me so well-adjusted.

FLY: Well, I'll be going. (*INTO COMPUTER*) Come in blue leader. This is blue bird. Yes, yes, my mission is complete. She is not only a well-established Christian, but she knows how to defend herself and her faith. Boy, does she ever. Over and out. (*HE EXITS*)

How To Give Away Your Faith

Theme
We are told to witness to others, but it's not so easy. Where do we begin? A good place is with our friends.

Summary
Two old friends talk about how to witness to a stranger.

Playing Time	3 minutes
Setting	Anywhere good friends meet
Props	None
Costumes	Whatever you decide
Cast	GOOBER — Like his name
	JONK — His friend

GOOBER: (*ENTERS ALONG WITH JONK. THEY STAND BACK TO BACK IN PROFILE*) Well, you did it again.

JONK: That's good.

GOOBER: No. That's bad.

JONK: Bad?

GOOBER: Bad!

JONK: Well, I did it again.

GOOBER: Yes, you did.

JONK: What did I do?

GOOBER: You made me look like a fool.

JONK: I did?

GOOBER: Yes, you did.

JONK: How?

GOOBER: You know very well how.

JONK: I do?

GOOBER: Yes, you do.

JONK: I do? Oh, yes, of course I do.

GOOBER: I was talking with that girl.

JONK: And you looked like a fool.

GOOBER: Not at first I didn't.

JONK: Later, then.

GOOBER: Yes, later. You know very well when.

JONK: I do? Oh, yes, of course I do — later.

GOOBER: Yes, later — later.

JONK: Later.

GOOBER: Later, when you came over — Buttinski.

JONK: Buttinski?

GOOBER: Buttinski. That's you.

JONK: Buttinski!

GOOBER: Yes. That's you. I was getting along fine without you.

JONK: You were?

GOOBER: I was. I was witnessing my faith.

JONK: Oh, that's what you were trying to do.

GOOBER: (*TURNING TOWARD JONK*) I wasn't trying ...

JONK: (*TURNING TOWARD GOOBER*) That's what I thought.

GOOBER: What's what you thought?

JONK: That's what I thought. You weren't trying.

GOOBER: I didn't mean that.

JONK: I always say what I mean. Maybe you should too.

GOOBER: You just made me look like a fool. That's all I know.

JONK: That's all you know?

GOOBER: You know what I mean.

JONK: No. Not really. I always say what I mean. Maybe you should too.

GOOBER: I do. I mean I try to. Anyway, you made me look like a fool when I was talking to that girl — witnessing my faith.

JONK: Later, you looked like a fool.

183

GOOBER: Because you made me look like one.

JONK: A fool.

GOOBER: A fool. Yes, a fool. You made me look like one.

JONK: How?

GOOBER: How?

JONK: Yes, how? You looked like a fool — later. After — you know.

GOOBER: Buttinski.

JONK: Yes, after Buttinski. Later, after Buttinski. How did I have anything to do with it?

GOOBER: You made me look like a fool.

JONK: How?

GOOBER: I'll tell you how.

JONK: Tell me.

GOOBER: Yes, I'll tell you.

JONK: Tell me.

GOOBER: You said — whatever it was you said. You know.

JONK: I do? Yes, of course I do.

GOOBER: Of course. Made me look like a fool.

JONK: I said, "Are you a good friend?"

GOOBER: That was it. That was it.

JONK: That was it. That's what I said.

GOOBER: Made me look like a fool.

JONK: That was it.

GOOBER: Made me look like a fool. "Are you a good friend?" Made me look like a fool.

JONK: That was it.

GOOBER: Made me look like a fool. Of course I wasn't her good friend.

JONK: Why?

GOOBER: Why?

JONK: Why?

GOOBER: Why? I'll tell you why. I wasn't her good friend because I had just met her, Buttinski.

JONK: Just met her?

GOOBER: Just met her. And two minutes later ...

JONK: Later. After ...

GOOBER: After Buttinski, later. Two minutes later, we parted.

JONK: Parted.

GOOBER: Parted. Yes. Parted.

JONK: Parted.

GOOBER: Parted after two minutes. That's sad, isn't it?

JONK: Sad?

GOOBER: Sad. Yes. I liked her a lot.

JONK: Why is that sad?

GOOBER: Because I would have liked to get to know her.

JONK: Wait. I've got it.

GOOBER: You've got what?

JONK: I've got it.

GOOBER: What?

JONK: I didn't make you look like a fool.

GOOBER: You did.

JONK: No, I didn't. You are a fool.

GOOBER: What?

JONK: Yes. That's your answer. You are a fool.

GOOBER: I am?

JONK: Why, yes. Of course you are. You are a fool. Isn't that great?

GOOBER: Great?

JONK: Great! Isn't that great? You are a fool.

GOOBER: Will you stop saying that. You're my friend.

JONK: Of course I am. And I'm the only one who'll tell you. You are a fool.

GOOBER: Will you stop saying that?

JONK: No. It's good news. I didn't make you look like a fool. You are a fool.

GOOBER: That's just great. I'm a fool.

JONK: Glad to hear you admit it.

GOOBER: Why am I a fool — because I was witnessing my faith to that girl?

JONK: No. Witnessing your faith is great.

GOOBER: I did something right, then.

JONK: Barely.

GOOBER: I did though, something right.

JONK: Yes, you did.

GOOBER: So, why am I a fool?

JONK: You were not her good friend.

GOOBER: But I was trying to become her good friend.

JONK: No, you weren't. You are a fool, remember.

GOOBER: I remember.

JONK: A fool. Yes, a fool. You have to be a person's good friend first.

GOOBER: Before I witness my faith.

JONK: Yes, of course.

GOOBER: I was a fool.

JONK: Yes, but now you're not.

GOOBER: So, who can I witness to? I don't have any good friends.

JONK: Oh, yes, you do.

GOOBER: I do?

JONK: Yes, you do.

GOOBER: Who?

JONK: Me.

GOOBER: You? I could witness my faith to you?

JONK: Yes, of course.

GOOBER: Why? Why would I do that? You're already a Christian.

JONK: No, I'm not.

GOOBER: You're not? I didn't know you weren't a Christian.

JONK: Well, I'm not.

GOOBER: I am a fool. (*THEY EXIT ARM IN ARM*)

Forgive And Heal

Theme
Jesus is God and proves it by forgiving sin and healing.

Summary
A young boy has faith enough to get his paralyzed father to Jesus to be healed and to bring his mother to a believing faith.

Playing Time	3 minutes
Setting	A poor home in Capernaum
Props	None
Costumes	The time of Christ, poor
Cast	MOTHER — the poor wife of a paralyzed man
	THOMAS — her son
	HARETH — his father

MOTHER: (*AS THOMAS ENTERS*) Thomas, come here!

THOMAS: Yes, Mother.

MOTHER: You disobeyed me.

THOMAS: Yes, Mother, I did.

MOTHER: Why? Why did you leave this house when I told you not to?

THOMAS: I had to, Mother. I just had to see Jesus.

189

MOTHER: And you left your father unattended, to do what? Follow some preacher! I told you. Don't get your hopes up about Jesus.

THOMAS: Oh, Mother, my hopes are up.

MOTHER: Well, if they are you're going to be disappointed.

THOMAS: Not me, Mother. And you won't be either.

MOTHER: I've been disappointed so many times. It's a way of life with me.

THOMAS: Let me tell you about Jesus, Mother.

MOTHER: I don't want to hear about Jesus. Let me tell you about your poor father lying upstairs, probably wanting a drink of water and you not there to give it to him. Oh, you are a bad boy.

THOMAS: I went to Joash's house and Jesus was surrounded by all these people. All wanting to be healed.

MOTHER: I'm not listening to this.

THOMAS: And I couldn't even get in to see Jesus.

MOTHER: Well, there now. That serves you right. Jesus, if he was any good, would have told you your place was at home with your mother and your helpless father.

THOMAS: But I took Father with me.

MOTHER: What? You what? How could you take your father anywhere? Your father's paralyzed!

THOMAS: I got a couple of friends and we came home and took Father over to Joash's house. As I said, there were too many people, so we took Father up to their roof and tore a hole in the roof and let Father down into the house.

MOTHER: A hole in the roof. Oh, it gets worse.

THOMAS: Oh, no, Mother. It gets better.

MOTHER: How will we ever fix our neighbor's roof?

HARETH: (*ENTERS*) I'll build him a new roof. My son here and I.

MOTHER: Hareth! You're walking. You're up and walking. Here, sit down. How? How?

THOMAS: Jesus healed him. I've been trying to tell you, Mother.

MOTHER: Jesus did this?

HARETH: Yes, he did. And I don't need to sit. I'm as strong as I ever was.

MOTHER: But how?

THOMAS: Jesus told Father that his sins were forgiven.

HARETH: Let me tell it, Thomas. It's my healing.

THOMAS: All right, Father.

HARETH: Well, as I was lying in front of Jesus and he said that my sins were forgiven, I believed that he was God. I believed.

MOTHER: I guess anyone would believe that.

HARETH: Not anyone. Not the scribes.

THOMAS: They didn't say a word. But Jesus knew their hearts.

MOTHER: Who doesn't know their hearts?

HARETH: And Jesus said to them: Why are you turning these things over in your hearts? Which is easier to say to this paralyzed man — your sins are forgiven or rise up, take up your bed and walk?

THOMAS: And the scribes didn't say a word, did they, Father?

HARETH: No, they didn't. But Jesus did. Jesus said to the scribes that to prove that he had the authority to forgive sins he would heal me. He told me to rise and take my bed and go home. So here I am!

MOTHER: Here you are! Indeed you are!

THOMAS: See, I told you, Mother. Hope!

MOTHER: We do have hope. We really do. Jesus is really the Messiah. The Son of God and our Lord.

HARETH: Let's go, son. We have a roof to repair.

To The Doctor

Theme

The lack of unity in the Body of Christ. The new wineskin is not prepared for the new wine.

Summary

Jesus goes to the doctor with some complaints about his body. He doesn't have the control over his body that he used to have.

Playing Time	3 minutes
Setting	A doctor's office
Props	Nurse — file folder, thermometer
Costumes	Doctor — white lab coat
	Nurse — white uniform
	Jesus — bandages, dark glasses, wheelchair
Cast	DOCTOR
	NURSE
	JESUS

DOCTOR: (*ENTERS ALONG WITH NURSE*) Miss Williams, is the next patient ready?

NURSE: (*HANDING THE DOCTOR THE FILE FOLDER*) Yes, Doctor, I'll bring him right in. Here are his records.

DOCTOR: Ah, yes. I remember this one. Remarkable. Quite extraordinary.

NURSE: He's in bad shape today.

DOCTOR: Well, let's see what's wrong.

NURSE: (*EXITING*) I'll bring him right in.

DOCTOR: Amazing patient. I always enjoy talking to him. (*NURSE ENTERS WITH JESUS IN WHEELCHAIR*) What in the world happened to you?

JESUS: It's my body. I been having a lot of trouble with it.

DOCTOR: I can see that. You used to be in such good shape — perfect condition. You had a powerful body once.

JESUS: Yes, I did once.

DOCTOR: You had good coordination. What happened to your eyes? (*NURSE STICKS THERMOMETER IN JESUS' MOUTH*)

JESUS: My eyes? Oh, the glasses. I can't stand bright lights any more.

DOCTOR: Let's take a look. (*TAKES JESUS' GLASSES OFF*) Now, look up. Down. Left. Right. When did you first start to have problems with your eyes?

JESUS: My eyes seem to do what they want to do.

DOCTOR: Can't you control your eyes?

JESUS: No, I can't. I have things I want to read, things to look at, but my eyes don't seem to follow the commands that my head is sending them.

DOCTOR: This is very strange. What do your eyes look at?

JESUS: Pornography. All types of horrible things.

DOCTOR: And you can't stop it?

JESUS: I can't seem to. But it's not just my eyes.

DOCTOR: Other parts of your body are affected?

JESUS: It seems that my entire body is affected. My feet go where I don't want them to go. My hands are often doing harmful things.

DOCTOR: And you can't get the different parts of your body to work together?

JESUS: You know, it's strange. Sometimes I can and sometimes I can't.

DOCTOR: But most of the time they are not working together. Is that correct?

JESUS: Right. They do work together but it's usually something I don't want them to do.

DOCTOR: It seems like your hands and feet have a mind of their own.

JESUS: It does seem that way, doesn't it? Is there anything you can do?

DOCTOR: I don't know if I can help you or not.

JESUS: You can't give me any hope?

DOCTOR: Well, no, I can't. We could try some medicine.

JESUS: You seem hesitant.

DOCTOR: I'm not sure it will work.

JESUS: What do I do?

DOCTOR: Well, I don't know exactly. There's probably no hope.

JESUS: None?

DOCTOR: Unless ...

JESUS: Yes?

DOCTOR: Do you pray?

JESUS: In my condition that's about all I can do. Yes, I pray a lot.

DOCTOR: It might do some good.

JESUS: Well, I'm certainly no good as I am.

DOCTOR: True.

JESUS: Well, that's it, then — prayer.

DOCTOR: Yes. That's it. (*NURSE ENTERS*)

JESUS: Well, that's what I'll do then.

DOCTOR: Try to keep going.

JESUS: I'll try. (*NURSE WHEELS JESUS OUT*)

DOCTOR: (*LOOKING AT FILE*) I certainly hope his condition improves. Nice guy. A name you don't hear too often anymore — Jesus. (*EXITS*)

What Say?

Theme
Grace is the basis for keeping the Sabbath day holy.

Summary
John and Peter, two disciples, harass the storyteller as he is reading a passage.

Playing Time	3 minutes
Setting	Your church
Props	None
Costumes	Storyteller — contemporary
	Disciples — suggestions of first century costumes
Cast	JOHN — a disciple
	PETER — another one
	STORYTELLER — a storyteller

STORYTELLER: (*ENTERS, STANDS CENTER STAGE, AND READS FROM THE KING JAMES BIBLE*) And it came to pass ... (*DISCIPLES ENTER AND PASS IN FRONT OF STORYTELLER*)

PETER: Pardon me. May I pass?

STORYTELLER: Why, yes, of course.

JOHN: Mind if I pass?

STORYTELLER: No, no. Go right ahead.

JOHN: He's very nice, don't you think?

PETER: Yes, very nice. I agree.

JOHN: (*TO STORYTELLER*) You're doing a very nice job.

STORYTELLER: Thank you. May I continue?

PETER: Certainly. We're waiting.

JOHN: We're hanging on every word.

STORYTELLER: Very well, I shall. He went through the cornfields on the Sabbath day; and his disciples began, as they went, to pluck the ears of corn.

PETER: Wait. Wait just a minute.

STORYTELLER: What's wrong?

PETER: What's wrong? I'll tell you what's wrong. You said corn.

STORYTELLER: Why, yes. I did. What's the matter with that?

PETER: It wasn't corn. It was wheat, if memory serves.

JOHN: Yes. If memory serves.

STORYTELLER: Your memory, I assume.

PETER: Most assuredly, my memory.

JOHN: And mine, too. And OUR memory serves.

PETER: Yes, our memory ALWAYS serves.

JOHN: ALWAYS!

STORYTELLER: Well, that's nice, but my Bible says corn.

PETER: But I'm telling you it was wheat. Don't you think we'd know the difference between corn and wheat?

JOHN: (*EXAGGERATING AND ACTING IT OUT*) Here, in my one hand I have a GREAT BIG ear of corn. And in my other hand I have a REALLY LITTLE grain of wheat. I wonder what the difference is? GREAT BIG ear of corn — REALLY LITTLE grain of wheat. BIG — LITTLE; CORN — WHEAT.

PETER: Yes, and another thing, there was no such thing as corn in those days.

JOHN: Yes, I wish there would have been. We had to eat REALLY LITTLE grains of wheat. I'd much rather have been eating GREAT BIG ears of corn.

PETER: So would I.

STORYTELLER: All right. Is that settled? I'll say wheat. All right?

JOHN: Yes, that's good — wheat.

STORYTELLER: All right, then. "And the Pharisees said unto him, Behold, why do they on the Sabbath day that which is not lawful?"

PETER: You know, I never knew what the Pharisees were talking about, did you?

JOHN: No, I never did. I just smiled a lot and nodded my head. (*JOHN AND PETER BEGIN TO SMILE AND NOD THEIR HEADS*)

STORYTELLER: "And Jesus said unto them, Have ye never read what David did?"

PETER: King David.

JOHN: He meant King David.

PETER: Yes, he did. I don't think that's very clear. But he did mean King David.

JOHN: Yes, he certainly did.

STORYTELLER: King David. That's good then. King David. Yes, King David. To continue: "When KING DAVID had need, and was an hungered, he and they that were with him?"

PETER: An hungered. (*HE LAUGHS*)

JOHN: And was an hungered. (*HE LAUGHS*)

STORYTELLER: Is everything all right?

PETER: (*STILL LAUGHING*) Oh, sure, go on.

JOHN: (*LAUGHING UNCONTROLLABLY*) And was an hungered.

STORYTELLER: "How he — KING DAVID went into the house of God in the days of Abiathar the high priest, and did eat the shewbread, which is not lawful to eat but for the priests, and gave also to them which were with him?" Everything all right?

PETER: Sure. Go on.

JOHN: He's very nice but a bit slow, don't you think?

PETER: He's all right.

STORYTELLER: "And Jesus said unto them ..."

JOHN: Here it is, then.

PETER: Finally, we get to it.

STORYTELLER: "The Sabbath was made for man and not man for the Sabbath."

PETER: He said a mouthful there, didn't he?

JOHN: And he said it very well, too.

PETER: Very well, indeed. I don't know if I could have done half so well.

JOHN: I think you could have.

PETER: Well, possibly. But I KNOW you could have.

JOHN: Thank you.

PETER: I like this last bit, don't you?

JOHN: Very much. It's my favorite. I can hardly wait.

PETER: Well, let's let him do it, shall we?

JOHN: Yes, let's.

STORYTELLER: Thank you. "Therefore the Son of Man is Lord also of the Sabbath."

JOHN: (*APPLAUDING*) Good. Good.

PETER: (*APPLAUDING*) I think it was excellent. Superb, even. (*PETER AND JOHN EXIT CONGRATULATING EACH OTHER, LEAVING THE STORYTELLER TO WANDER OFFSTAGE ALONE*)

Edenville

Theme

Satan is working today in the world as it was in the beginning. We have to know our enemy in order to resist.

Summary

What if God had created a city instead of a garden?

Playing Time	3 minutes
Setting	The new world
Props	Matches, ladder, flashlight, sign, candy bar
Costumes	Performance costumes
Cast	GOD
	ADAM
	EVE
	SATAN

GOD: *(AN ACTOR HOLDS A SIGN THAT READS "SITE OF EDENVILLE." GOD ENTERS, STROLLS AROUND CREATING)* What shall I create today? I know, I'll create a city for myself. Let there be light. *(AN ACTOR STRIKES A MATCH)* Let there be a skyscraper. *(AN ACTOR CLIMBS A LADDER AND TURNS ON A FLASHLIGHT)* Let there be a gas station. *(AN ACTOR STICKS A FINGER IN HIS EAR AND SAYS "DING")* And let there be a vending machine. *(AN ACTOR BECOMES A VENDING MACHINE)* Hmm. This city needs something. I know what this city needs. This city needs a man. *(GOD PICKS UP SOME IMAGINARY DUST AND BLOWS INTO IT. MAN COMES TO LIFE. "SITE OF EDENVILLE" SIGN IS CHANGED TO READ "EDENVILLE, POP. 1")*

ADAM: (*COMING TO LIFE*) Oh, God, this is wonderful.

GOD: This city has been created for your pleasure. You're in charge of everything. (*GOD BEGINS TO EXIT*)

ADAM: But, God, I think I'm lonely.

GOD: Then I'll create a woman for you. (*ADAM GROANS AND HOLDS HIS SIDE. GOD LEADS WOMAN TO ADAM AND PLACES HER HAND IN HIS. ADAM'S GROAN TURNS TO AN "AHH" OF ADMIRATION. POPULATION CHANGES TO "TWO." GOD EXITS*) Now, you're both in charge of this city. One command I leave with you, you can eat anywhere in the city except from the vending machine. I repeat, take no food from this vending machine. Enjoy yourselves.

ADAM: I'm tired. It's been a hard first day. I think I'll take a nap. (*HE SLEEPS. EVE LOOKS AROUND AT CREATION WHO WAVES TO HER*)

SATAN: (*ENTERS*) Hello, there, little girl.

EVE: Hello.

SATAN: Nice place you have here.

EVE: Yeah, real nice.

SATAN: Did I hear that God fellow say that you couldn't eat any food from that vending machine?

EVE: Yes, that's what he said, but he said we could eat anywhere else we wanted to.

SATAN: That's a bunch of hooey. Do you know why He doesn't want you to eat from that vending machine? Do you? Because He knows if you do you'll be as smart as He is. Go ahead, it doesn't cost anything. Go ahead. (*EVE PUSHES FIST OF VENDING MACHINE AND THE OTHER HAND PRODUCES A CANDY BAR. SHE TAKES IT AND EATS A BITE*)

EVE: (*ROUSING ADAM*) Adam. Adam. You've got to try this.

ADAM: What is it?

EVE: It's a candy bar.

ADAM: You didn't get that from the vending machine, did you?

EVE: Sure, I did, but it's all right. I'm still here. Come on, try it.

ADAM: (*TASTING IT*) Mmmm. That is good.

GOD: Ahem. (*ADAM AND EVE HIDE*) Where are you two? (*ENTERS.*) I know, you took food from the vending machine, didn't you.

ADAM: She made me do it.

GOD: Never mind. You both disobeyed me. Now, you're both banned from Edenville forever. Now go. (*ADAM AND EVE EXIT AND GOD CHANGES SIGN FROM "2" TO "0"*) Oh well, how about plan B?

Growth

Theme

In the Kingdom of God beginnings are always small but can grow with God's help.

Summary

Carol, a college student, is taking a botany test and not doing well, but her teacher receives a lesson when she teaches about the mustard seed.

Playing Time	3 1/2 minutes
Setting	A college classroom
Props	A potted mustard plant
Costumes	Appropriate for the college classroom
Time	Now
Cast	PROFESSOR — A botany teacher
	CAROL — his student

PROFESSOR: (*CARRYING A POTTED PLANT*) And now for the last plant, Miss Simpson. I hope you can identify this one. You've missed all the others.

CAROL: I'm ready, Professor Greewalt.

PROFESSOR: Very good, what plant is this?

CAROL: I can't remember.

PROFESSOR: Look at the leaves.

CAROL: (*INSPECTING THE PLANT CLOSELY*) Tomato.

PROFESSOR: No, not a tomato plant. Observe the structure of the stem.

CAROL: Pepper.

PROFESSOR: Quit guessing. You should know this plant.

CAROL: I don't know.

PROFESSOR: I'm disappointed in you, Miss Simpson. You don't know your plants, do you?

CAROL: I couldn't get that one.

PROFESSOR: You couldn't get any of them. A mustard plant, Miss Simpson. You haven't been studying, have you?

CAROL: I had a big test in theology yesterday.

PROFESSOR: And you studied theology instead of botany, is that correct?

CAROL: Yes, sir, that's what happened, that along with helping at the homeless shelter.

PROFESSOR: Helping at a homeless shelter? How can that further your career? Can you tell me if there is any reason I should give you a passing grade in this course, Miss Simpson?

CAROL: Yes, sir. There is one.

PROFESSOR: And what is that?

CAROL: (*TAKING THE PLANT FROM THE PROFESSOR*) I know what the mustard seed represents.

PROFESSOR: I also know what it represents — your failing grade.

CAROL: No, no. The mustard seed represents the Kingdom of God.

PROFESSOR: You're a little confused, Miss Simpson. First of all, there is no God, and secondly, this is botany, a science, not theology, a fantasyland.

CAROL: I just got an "A" on my theology test.

PROFESSOR: A tremendous waste of time.

CAROL: Nevertheless, I do know something about the plant.

PROFESSOR: Surprise me.

CAROL: It's the greatest of all herbs, so big in fact that the birds can nest in it.

PROFESSOR: You did study. What else do you know?

CAROL: The mustard seed is really small, trifling, you might say.

PROFESSOR: Very true. It is insignificant.

CAROL: And yet it is of great significance.

PROFESSOR: A riddle?

CAROL: Not really. It's like the Kingdom of God.

PROFESSOR: The Kingdom of God again.

CAROL: You start out small in the Kingdom of God, like the mustard seed, and grow into greater service.

PROFESSOR: Greater service?

CAROL: Yes, to God and to others, like the birds in the mustard bush. The bush provides them shelter.

PROFESSOR: And you think that this theological mumbo jumbo will get you a good grade in botany?

CAROL: Maybe not. But it's worth a lot more to me.

PROFESSOR: What about your grades? Why are you so concerned about God? What if I told you there was no God?

CAROL: You said that before, but it didn't change the fact that God created the mustard seed.

PROFESSOR: Can you prove that?

CAROL: Of course not, but science, and botany in particular, doesn't know why you stick a mustard seed in the ground and a mustard bush grows.

PROFESSOR: At least the botanist can identify the mustard plant.

CAROL: What if there is a God? Wouldn't it be more important to identify Him?

PROFESSOR: What about your grade in botany?

CAROL: I can improve that. What about your grade?

PROFESSOR: I beg your pardon.

CAROL: If there is a God, what kind of grade will you be getting?

Calming The Storm

Theme

Does Jesus know and care about our everyday problems that seem so big to us?

Summary

Things are overwhelming and Claudia can't cope.

Playing Time	3 minutes
Setting	Claudia and Paul's home
Props	Telephone
Costumes	Contemporary, casual
Time	Now
Cast	CLAUDIA — wife
	PAUL — husband

CLAUDIA: (*ENTERS IN A STATE OF AGITATION. SHE COUGHS PERIODICALLY*) I am swamped!

PAUL: (*OFFSTAGE*) What?

CLAUDIA: It's like I'm drowning.

PAUL: I put him outside.

CLAUDIA: I can't stand it. (*CRYING*) Paul, I'm really hurting here.

PAUL: What? I can't hear you.

CLAUDIA: I lost my mother's death certificate. I don't know where it is.

PAUL: I can't hear you. I'll be there in a minute.

CLAUDIA: Lord, I can't stand it. I just can't stand it. What's happening? Why am I having all this trouble? Why aren't you listening to me? Lord, don't you care that I'm drowning? I'm drowning here.

PAUL: (*ENTERS. FINISHING GETTING DRESSED FOR WORK*) I put the cat outside. Hey, which tie goes with this shirt?

CLAUDIA: I really can't stand it. I really need help. I'm drowning here.

PAUL: (*HUGS HER*) Claudia, what is it?

CLAUDIA: It's just everything. Just everything. It's like nothing is going right for me. Doesn't God care about us? I'm sick. I've been sick now for two weeks. The doctor doesn't seem to know what's wrong with me. It's like no one cares. I can't get well. And now I can't find my mother's death certificate. I had two extra death certificates made for the court and I sent one with that insurance claim and I put the other one right here on the bed and now I can't find it. The washing machine is leaking water. We can't afford to buy a washing machine. What is this? What's happening? Oh, Paul, where is God when things get tough? When you really need Him where is He? Doesn't He care about our little problems?

PAUL: Did you pray about it?

CLAUDIA: No.

PAUL: I love you, Claudia. (*PRAYING*) Jesus, right now just comfort Claudia. Hold her in your arms just like I'm holding her

211

now. You are loved, Claudia. I love you. Jesus hasn't forgotten us. He knows exactly where that lost death certificate is. It's not lost to him. He cares. He'll see us through this. He will. You'll see.

CLAUDIA: I don't know. I called the lady at the insurance office. Wouldn't you know it, she wasn't there.

PAUL: Probably on break.

CLAUDIA: I need some answers.

PAUL: I know. Jesus will give us answers. He cares. You'll see. Just relax and hang in there. You'll get well. The doctor said you would.

CLAUDIA: I know what he said. It's just that it's taking so long. I can't sleep at night. I cough all night. I'm so tired.

PAUL: Did you eat breakfast?

CLAUDIA: No, no, I didn't. I was making that call and then she wasn't there and then I couldn't find my mom's death certificate and I'm so tired and the washing machine and ...

PAUL: I'll tell you what. We're going to pray. How does that sound?

CLAUDIA: Yeah.

PAUL: Dear Jesus, we know down deep in our hearts that you care for us. We know how much you care for us. Would you please show Claudia where that death certificate is and, Lord, you created the metal that went into making that washing machine, and you created the people who created that machine, so could you get it fixed, please? Or if it's real easy, show me how to fix it. Oh, Lord, could you please heal Claudia? I love her so much. I hate to see her sick. She's so miserable and can't sleep. Give her a day of rest, please, Lord. And when she wakes up have her feeling a little better, please. Thanks a lot, Jesus. We love you. We're just in deep water right now. We need you to rescue us. Amen.

CLAUDIA: Thanks, Hon. I love you. You helped. I was really low. You really helped.

PAUL: Well, I'll get you some breakfast if you'll pick a tie for me to wear. (*EXITS*) And then you're going to take a nap. (*PHONE RINGS*)

CLAUDIA: (*ANSWERING IT*) Yes? Oh, good. Good. All right. I was wondering where it was. Thanks. Thanks a lot. Bye. (*HANGS UP*) Thank you, Jesus.

PAUL: What? (*ENTERS*)

CLAUDIA: That was the insurance company. I mailed them both death certificates. They're going to mail me the extra one.

PAUL: (*THEY HUG*) You see. Jesus takes care of us. What about my tie?

CLAUDIA: Did you pray about it? (*THEY EXIT*)

The Healer

Theme
Jesus is available to all who want him.

Summary
Elisheba is an outcast and needs a physical healing. A monologue.

Playing Time	3 minutes
Setting	Your church
Props	None
Costumes	Peasant, of first century, Christian
Time	Now
Cast	ELISHEBA — a woman who needs healing

ELISHEBA: (*ENTERS*) To me, there seem to be two classes of people in the world — those who have hope and those who don't. I've been a member of both classes.

I'm called Elisheba. Let me tell you about being hopeless and why I now have hope. This is a personal story. Very personal. I haven't shared this story with many. But I'll share it with you. I think I can trust you.

For twelve years I didn't smile. That's a long time to be so grim, I know, but you'll understand when I tell you what my problem was.

It was a delicate problem. You see, I had a son born dead and because of that I had a constant flow of blood. That fact excluded me from temple worship and I was cut off from everyone. I was unclean. I couldn't even sleep with my husband. No one could touch me and I could not touch others. It was the law.

Twelve years — alone. Twelve years of pain, misery, frustration, depression, and humiliation. My nights and days were occupied with being alone. Ceremonially unclean, that's what the law said. I was ceremonially unclean. What it meant was I was an outcast, unwanted, unloved, a burden, and alone with my hurt. My affliction was constantly with me.

I desperately wanted to be loved. I longed for love. I fantasized about love. I remembered how it used to be and I despaired how it could never be again. That's the thing that hurt most. I had no one to love me.

I lived with my husband and mother-in-law but was not allowed to be with them, and they didn't want to be with me anyway.

My husband had spent all his money on helping me find a cure for my bleeding, and my mother-in-law cursed me and blamed me for all our troubles. My husband wanted a son and all he got was poverty and a wife who was a burden.

I can still hear my mother-in-law yelling at me: "We expected an heir and we got death. Cursed! That's what you are, cursed. The evil curse you brought on this house will never be lifted. You're evil. What kind of a wife are you? You're nothing. Nothing, but evil, and I hate you! You've ruined my son and disgraced our house and I hate you. I hate you!"

I screamed too. I used to scream my prayers to God: Oh, God, where are you? I used to go to the temple every day but I haven't been for twelve years. Your laws won't let me talk to you. Those who need you most cannot even come close to you to tell you of their need. What kind of God are you? A God of the people who are well and whole. But what about the rest of us? We need you too. I need you. I need you so much. Oh, Lord God in heaven, I need you now.

There's no hope for me. No hope — unless — unless — I heard a teacher, a prophet they say. His name is Jesus. I heard him teach twice, once in a discussion with some of the elders and once when he taught a large crowd. Of course I couldn't be part of the crowd, but I did get close enough to hear him. He said he loved us. I liked hearing that. I needed to hear that.

He said if we believed in him we would be saved. Saved from what? I certainly needed to be saved from my bleeding. Maybe he could heal me. Maybe. He's my only hope. I'll just go and ask him to heal me.

No. It's not possible. I would never get close enough. No one would ever let me get that close. I couldn't ask him to heal me. That would make him unclean. It's impossible.

What if I could brush up against him on the street? No, he'd still be unclean. Maybe just touching him would make me well. But, what if — I could just touch his garment. He won't know it and I'll be healed.

I roamed the streets of Capernaum for days, being careful not to be recognized. Two long weeks I searched for him, only to find out he'd gone on a preaching tour across the Sea of Galilee.

When he returned I again took to the streets to find him. One day, after a long day of walking up one street and down another, I heard a lot of noise behind me.

It's a crowd coming down the street — fast. My heart leapt. Could it be? I guessed the answer. It had to be him. He's the only person who could draw a crowd like that.

The crowd pushed past me. Here was my chance, but before I realized it I was pushed against the wall and I knew I had missed him. I missed him!

But, no, there he is! There. I see the back of his head. If I run fast. I don't know. I haven't run in years. But I must reach him. I must. I don't care if I touch anyone now. I must touch him! I have to. Get out of my way. Out of my way! I must get to Jesus. He's my only hope. Move! I must reach him.

He stopped. Good, he stopped. I can catch up. He's talking to some official who is kneeling at his feet. He's distracted. Good.

I'll just kneel here and just reach out and touch. Just a little more. Slowly, quietly, ever so softly. There, I did it. Just a touch. Just a touch.

Oh, Lord, I can feel it. I — I — I'm healed. I know it. I feel it. I'm healed. I must slip away now. Slip back into the crowd. Back home.

But, he's turning toward me. Oh no. It can't be. He's asking his friends who touched him. Oh no.

Lord, Lord, forgive me, Lord. I only wanted to — to be healed. I am unclean and now I've defiled you, too.

I hear what you say, Lord. I do have a little faith. I had faith that you could heal me. Yes, I know. I can hold my head high now. Yes. I am a child of God. And your faithful servant, always.

Praise the Lord. That's exactly the way it happened. And on the eighth day I spent our last bit of money on two of the finest turtle doves for the offering. And what a celebration. My whole life was changed. The house of my husband is now a happy home. We all became followers of the Messiah, even my mother-in-law.

The Way It Works

Theme
How is our forgiveness related to Jesus?

Summary
Three people discuss Jesus and the fact that he is telling people their sins are forgiven. How can anyone forgive sins? Who is Jesus and what right does he have to say these things?

Playing Time	3 minutes
Setting	Your church
Props	None
Costumes	Peasant, of first century, Christian
Time	The time of Jesus
Cast	JOEL
	NATHAN
	DANIEL

JOEL: (*ENTERS ALONG WITH NATHAN AND DANIEL*) Where did this man get these things?

NATHAN: Jesus?

DANIEL: You know who we mean. Yes, Jesus.

NATHAN: What things are you talking about?

JOEL: The things he teaches. We've never had a teacher like this.

NATHAN: None of us has ever heard such teaching.

DANIEL: I'm not so sure we want this teaching. His teaching will lead to anarchy.

NATHAN: Anarchy? How will "Your sins are forgiven" lead to anarchy?

JOEL: No one can forgive sins. No one. If a person says, "Your sins are forgiven," he must be a madman. That's it. He's a madman. "Your sins are forgiven." C'mon. If I came up to you and said, "Your sins are forgiven," what would you do?

NATHAN: I'd shake your hand and think, "My sins are forgiven, fantastic. I'm free. I'm clean."

JOEL: Okay, okay, I didn't really mean that. Calm down.

NATHAN: Anyone would be glad to have his sins forgiven.

DANIEL: Of course, if you're talking about sins against someone else. But he's not talking about that.

NATHAN: Who says he doesn't mean that?

JOEL: No. He means that you are forgiven of all your sins. All your sins. Get it?

NATHAN: That's even better. Imagine that all your sins are forgiven. That's fantastic.

JOEL: Of course it would be fantastic — if it were true.

DANIEL: We all have our sins forgiven now.

JOEL: Of course we do. On the day of sacrifice.

NATHAN: Yes, they are. Our sins are all forgiven on the day of sacrifice.

DANIEL: Well, then, why do we need this guy telling us our sins are forgiven?

NATHAN: How long?

DANIEL: How long what?

NATHAN: How long are your sins forgiven?

DANIEL: What difference does that make?

JOEL: Until the next day of atonement, I guess.

DANIEL: Yeah. Next year. Our sins are forgiven every year.

NATHAN: Why?

JOEL: Because Moses said so.

DANIEL: Yeah. Right. And God spoke directly to Moses.

NATHAN: Right. He did. But why do we get our sins forgiven every year on the day of sacrifice?

JOEL: Because we need it every year.

DANIEL: Right. We sin again and so we need forgiven again.

NATHAN: How soon?

JOEL: How soon, what?

NATHAN: I mean, how soon do we need to be forgiven after we've been forgiven?

DANIEL: As soon as we sin, I guess. I don't know.

NATHAN: How soon would that be?

DANIEL: I don't know. It could be anytime, I guess.

NATHAN: The next day?

DANIEL: Yes. I guess so, sure.

NATHAN: The next hour?

DANIEL: Sure, I guess so. A person could ...

NATHAN: The next minute?

DANIEL: Uh ...

NATHAN: Well, could a person sin the next minute after being forgiven on the day of atonement?

DANIEL: I don't know. Yes, it's possible. I guess it's possible.

NATHAN: How about the next second?

JOEL: Now, wait a minute. What's the point of this?

NATHAN: I was just thinking, what if you sinned the next second after being forgiven, what good is the forgiveness? You'd have to wait an whole year to be clear of sin again. To have that great feeling of freedom from guilt. A whole year. You'd carry a load of sin a whole year, and then after being forgiven you'd have to wait another year.

JOEL: Well, that's the system. That's the way it works.

NATHAN: Maybe not.

221

JOEL: Of course that's the way it works. That's the system. If it was good enough for Moses ...

DANIEL: Unless you keep the law, and then you wouldn't sin at all.

JOEL: But no one can do that.

DANIEL: Some people claim they can, but we know they can't. We know human nature. No one can keep the law for a whole day, let alone a whole year.

JOEL: So, we're all sinners without any hope of having our sins forgiven.

NATHAN: And yet Jesus is telling people their sins are forgiven.

DANIEL: How can he do that?

NATHAN: I've been thinking about that. Don't the scriptures say there is no forgiveness of sin without the shedding of blood?

JOEL: Yes. The scriptures say that, but Jesus is not a priest. He cannot make sacrifices.

DANIEL: And even if he could, it would only be for a second until we sinned again.

JOEL: We're back where we started.

NATHAN: But what if there was a sacrifice that would continue forever?

JOEL: Impossible.

NATHAN: With God all things are possible. Or else God is not God.

JOEL: If it's a sacrifice that lasts forever it would have to be a sacrifice that God makes.

DANIEL: Because only God lasts forever.

JOEL: But where would God get an animal that lives forever so it would be a sacrifice that continues forever?

DANIEL: Angels?

NATHAN: No. God created the angels so they don't live forever.

JOEL: It's just impossible.

NATHAN: What if God Himself was the sacrifice?

JOEL: How could God sacrifice Himself?

NATHAN: I don't know exactly, but Jesus is telling people their sins are forgiven.

DANIEL: This is too much for me.

NATHAN: Jesus might have something there. He does miracles. He must be a prophet. Let's listen to him and watch him and find out.

Change

Theme
God will supply all our needs.

Summary
Two disciples talk about the upcoming missions trip and how Jesus limits their dependence on things.

Playing Time	3 1/2 minutes
Setting	Anywhere disciples meet
Props	List
Costumes	Contemporary, casual
Time	Now
Cast	MATTHEW — a disciple
	THADDEUS — another disciple

MATTHEW: (*ENTERS ALONG WITH THADDEUS*) Did you prepare your missions support newsletter?

THADDEUS: I tore it up.

MATTHEW: How are you going to go on a missions trip if you don't send out your letter?

THADDEUS: Read this. (*HANDING MATTHEW A LIST*)

MATTHEW: What's this?

THADDEUS: You weren't at the meeting. This is what Jesus told us to take.

MATTHEW: And not to take.

THADDEUS: Right.

MATTHEW: (*READING*) "A walking stick"? I don't have a walking stick.

THADDEUS: You might need one.

MATTHEW: "No food"? What about snacks? The airlines don't give very good snacks anymore.

THADDEUS: I don't think you'll find airlines mentioned anywhere.

MATTHEW: "No bag"? What am I supposed to carry my clothes in? He doesn't mention a briefcase. I need my briefcase and my daytimer — my laptop, printer, fax. No bag? Are you sure you took good notes?

THADDEUS: Yes, it's right. He went over it twice.

MATTHEW: "No money"? I don't carry much anyway. I put it all on plastic. Then you have a record. I do need something for tips, though. "No extra pair of shoes"? What about those dinner parties? How would it look wearing hiking boots to a dinner party?

THADDEUS: That's pretty well covered.

MATTHEW: "No extra clothes"? Well, I guess there won't be any dinner parties.

THADDEUS: It looks that way.

MATTHEW: "When you enter a house, stay there until you leave." That sounds reasonable. But look at this: "If any place won't accept you or listen to you, shake off the dust of your feet as you leave it." Wow! What would Miss Manners say to that? Dusting your feet in public. Hmm. I don't know. Do you think he's a little out of touch?

THADDEUS: Well, we should follow the list, I guess.

MATTHEW: Look at this. It says he gave us authority over unclean spirits. That's nice. I like that. But what about this last part? We have to preach that people should repent and cast out demons and anoint people with oil and heal the sick. Hey, I'm not called to that.

THADDEUS: Aren't we all called to that?

MATTHEW: Not me. So, I don't have to do all this stuff on the list. I'm sending out my own letter. See you on the mission field.

THADDEUS: I think I'll do what Jesus said.

1/23/06

Lost Your Lunch

Theme

Just by being ourselves and open to God's will we can be a part of God's miracles.

Summary

Dov has arrived home late at night having lost the wood he was taking to town to sell and the lunch he was going to eat. He tells his wife of the miracle of hearing Jesus teach and seeing him work a miracle.

Playing Time	4 minutes
Setting	Galilean peasant home
Props	None
Costumes	Peasant of Jesus' time
Time	The time of Jesus
Cast	DOV — a Galilean
	SHUSHANA — his wife

SHUSHANA: (*ENTERS ALONG WITH DOV*) It's late.

DOV: (*TAKING OFF OUTER GARMENT*) I know.

SHUSHANA: Did you get the money for the firewood?

DOV: No, I didn't.

SHUSHANA: Well, that's all right. You can sell it tomorrow. You can do anything.

DOV: Well, maybe not this time. I lost the wood.

SHUSHANA: What? Lost the wood? What are you saying?

DOV: I lost it all.

SHUSHANA: But, how? How can you lose a bundle of firewood that's at least as big as you are?

DOV: Well, I set it down when I heard Jesus was going to be in town.

SHUSHANA: Jesus. Oh, well, that explains it. You can get more wood to sell. You can do anything.

DOV: I sure can.

SHUSHANA: Did you eat all your lunch?

DOV: No. I lost my lunch.

SHUSHANA: You were sick?

DOV: No, no. I lost it.

SHUSHANA: Someone stole your lunch.

DOV: Nope.

SHUSHANA: I'll fix you something. You must be hungry.

DOV: I'm not hungry.

SHUSHANA: You must be. You lost your lunch. How did you lose your lunch?

DOV: I was so interested in what Jesus was saying that I just sat my lunch down somewhere and left it.

SHUSHANA: Then you must be hungry.

DOV: I'm not hungry. I ate.

SHUSHANA: You ate? You ate what?

DOV: You won't believe this. I ate my lunch.

SHUSHANA: What a riddle you are. You lost your lunch and yet you ate your lunch. You better tell me everything.

DOV: All right. I was on my way to town with the firewood and Elhana and Joash went running by me. They had heard that Jesus was in Chorazin and they were going to go listen to him.

SHUSHANA: I wish I would have been there. Were there a lot of people?

DOV: Were there a lot of people? There sure were. All of them running up the road to Chorazin. I left my wood beside the road and followed them.

SHUSHANA: That's something? Is that where you lost your lunch?

DOV: No. I still had my lunch with me. It was so exciting. Jesus and his disciples were coming by boat but we got there before he did.

SHUSHANA: What did Jesus do?

DOV: Well, he taught as usual, and he healed some people who were sick and then he fed us.

SHUSHANA: All of you?

DOV: All of us. We ate my lunch.

SHUSHANA: Who ate your lunch?

DOV: We all did. All the people who were there.

SHUSHANA: Everyone?

DOV: Everyone. It was a miracle. There must have been about five thousand men there, I suppose.

SHUSHANA: Five thousand. And you fed them with your little lunch? You can do anything. How did you feed all those people?

DOV: I didn't. Jesus did.

SHUSHANA: Well, tell me.

DOV: I guess someone found my lunch and gave it to Jesus. I don't know. All I know is that all those people were there and they were hungry. Me too. I was hungry. And then Jesus' disciples were passing out fish and bread, just like my little lunch. I had more than enough to eat. My own lunch! Everyone ate my lunch!

SHUSHANA: Jesus made enough to eat for five thousand from your little lunch. What a blessing.

DOV: It was really something. Thanks for caring enough for me to pack my lunch. Just think, if you hadn't packed my lunch all those people would have gone hungry today. You were a part of a miracle.

SHUSHANA: And you. Just think, you were part of a miracle too.

DOV: Me? What did I do?

SHUSHANA: You lost your lunch! You really can do anything.

Cardio-sclerosis

Theme

Many people's hearts are hardened. Jesus can cure the hardened heart, but only if the person wants it.

Summary

Mr. Green has a problem. His heart is hardened and the doctor says he can fix the problem if Mr. Green wants to take the necessary steps, but he doesn't want to.

Playing Time	4 minutes
Setting	A doctor's office
Props	File and clipboard
Costumes	Doctor — white lab coat
	Mr. Green — contemporary
Time	The present
Cast	DOCTOR
	MR. GREEN — the patient

DOCTOR: (*ENTERS ALONG WITH GREEN*) Well, Mr. Green, we're finished with your test.

GREEN: You've found the reason for my chest pains?

DOCTOR: Yes, we did.

GREEN: Well, what is it?

DOCTOR: You're terminal.

GREEN: Terminal?

DOCTOR: Terminal.

GREEN: Terminal!

DOCTOR: Terminal.

GREEN: I see. And what does that mean to me?

DOCTOR: It means you're going to die.

GREEN: I am?

DOCTOR: Definitely.

GREEN: How much...?

DOCTOR: Time? Everyone asks that. That depends.

GREEN: On what?

DOCTOR: On what you do about your lifestyle.

GREEN: I'll change. I swear I will. I've got a lot to live for.

DOCTOR: You do? Good.

GREEN: I'll do whatever you say. What's my condition?

DOCTOR: Cardio-sclerosis.

GREEN: Come again?

DOCTOR: Hard heart.

GREEN: Hard...?

233

DOCTOR: Hard heart.

GREEN: Hard heart. What does that mean, to me, I mean?

DOCTOR: I already told you, Mr. Green. You're terminal.

GREEN: So, you think I'm going to die.

DOCTOR: I know it.

GREEN: And there's nothing you can do — some medicine?

DOCTOR: I've done all I can do, Mr. Green. It's up to you now ... and God.

GREEN: God? Oh, yes, God. What's God got to do with this?

DOCTOR: Everything.

GREEN: You're not going to tell me to pray, are you? I don't ...

DOCTOR: I pray.

GREEN: That praying stuff's not for me. Aaugh! (*HE HAS A SHARP PAIN IN HIS CHEST*)

DOCTOR: Pain? (*MAKING NO ATTEMPT TO HELP BUT DOES SHOW CONCERN*)

GREEN: Yeah, Doc. Give me something!

DOCTOR: I just did.

GREEN: You just did? What are you talking about? Did I miss something? Here I am in a doctor's office in agony and I ask you for something to relieve this pain and you said you just gave me something.

DOCTOR: I suggested prayer.

GREEN: Nonsense. (*MORE PAIN*) Aaugh! Doc, give me something, please. This pain is too much!

DOCTOR: It will increase in intensity until you die.

GREEN: Give me something, please, Doc.

DOCTOR: All right. I will. Read your Bible.

GREEN: Cut the funny stuff, Doc. I'm a busy man. I don't have time to read the Bible. (*MORE PAIN*) Aaugh! Doc, Doc, do something.

DOCTOR: I told you already, I can't do anything for you, Mr. Green. You're terminal.

GREEN: Will you quit saying that?

DOCTOR: It's the truth. You're going to die, and painfully too, unless you change your lifestyle.

GREEN: I said I'll change. I'll walk in the mall — anything. Tell me what to do.

DOCTOR: Go to church.

GREEN: Do you mean walk to church?

DOCTOR: It doesn't matter how you get there, just go.

GREEN: I'll walk in the mall on Sunday mornings. That's the only time I have to spare — Sunday mornings. I certainly don't see how sitting in church on Sunday mornings could help my heart. (*MORE PAIN*) Aaugh!

DOCTOR: Do you know Jesus?

GREEN: I've got pain. It's killing me!

DOCTOR: That's what I've been trying to tell you.

GREEN: I came to see a doctor and I get a preacher.

DOCTOR: I guess you're just blessed. Jesus died so you wouldn't have to go through the pain of death.

GREEN: I need some painkillers.

DOCTOR: Jesus took the pain of death so you wouldn't have to die.

GREEN: Cut out the Jesus stuff. I don't want to hear it. (*MORE PAIN*) Aaugh! (*HE EXITS*)

DOCTOR: He wouldn't listen. He's going to die a horrible death. But he did it to himself. Hard heart is instantly curable. Instantly curable. All he has to do is turn to Jesus. (*SHE EXITS*)

Super Christian II

Theme

When we follow our own will instead of waiting on God we can become super-Christians and actually miss the better thing God has for us.

Summary

Super Christian is always on the job ready to make things right. It's just his perception that is a little off. The right place — the wrong person.

Playing Time	3 minutes
Setting	Some place near your church
Props	Handgun, case with ribbon, wallet, handbag, rope, bandanna
Costumes	Super Christian — a pair of blue pajamas and cape, "S.C." on the chest
Time	The present
Cast	BETH — a teenager
	AMY — another one
	ANNOUNCER
	PRIEST
	SUPER CHRISTIAN

ANNOUNCER: (*ENTERS AND SPEAKS INTO MICROPHONE*) Faster than a speeding bullet. More powerful than a mighty locomotive. Able to leap tall church buildings at a single bound. Look! Up in the air! It's a bird! It's a plane! No, it's Super Christian! Yes, Super Christian, who, disguised as a mild-mannered Sunday school teacher, wages a never-ending battle for peace, justice, and the Christian way. As our exciting adventure begins, Super Christian is just wrapping up a case.

SUPER CHRISTIAN: (*ACTUALLY WRAPPING A CASE WITH A NICE RIBBON*) This will look nice for Grandmother's birthday.

ANNOUNCER: While in another part of town ...

BETH: Maybe you ought to drive the getaway car this time.

AMY: You know I'm not old enough to drive. Besides, I like scaring people with this gun. (*PRODUCING GUN FROM POCKET*)

BETH: Okay, I'll drive. Here comes someone now. Ready?

AMY: (*PRIEST ENTERS. AMY SLIPS UP BEHIND HIM AND JAMS GUN IN HIS BACK*) Okay, you, reach for the sky. Now, hand over your wallet. (*PRIEST GIVES HER HIS WALLET AND AMY PUTS IT IN HER HANDBAG*)

PRIEST: You'll never get away with this.

AMY: That's what you think. We're the biggest ring of teenage criminals in this city. And now to tie you up. (*SHE BEGINS TO TIE HIS HANDS TOGETHER IN FRONT OF HIM*)

PRIEST: This is going to be your last job. Help! Help!

AMY: Enough of that. (*SHE TIES A BANDANNA AROUND HIS MOUTH AS A GAG*)

ANNOUNCER: While on the other side of town, Super Christian hears the call of distress with his super-hearing ear.

SUPER CHRISTIAN: (*LISTENING*) With my super-hearing ear, I just heard a call of distress. This will have to wait. (*HE TRIES TO TOSS CASE ASIDE BUT HE HAS TIED HIS FINGER INTO THE BOW. IT TAKES SOME MANIPULATION TO FREE HIMSELF*)

ANNOUNCER: Super Christian flies to the rescue ... very fast.

BETH: Making a fuss, eh? (*SHE HITS HIM WITH THE BAG. PRIEST GRABS BAG AND STAGGERS BACK FROM THE BLOW*)

AMY: Look out. Here comes Super Christian.

SUPER CHRISTIAN: (*COMING TO THE RESCUE VERY FAST*) This looks like a job for ... *Super Christian!* (*FLEXING HIS MUSCLES*) Aha! A purse snatcher. (*PRIEST MUMBLES THROUGH HIS GAG AND STAGGERS TOWARD SUPER CHRISTIAN*) And drunk, too. How disgraceful. (*AMY AND BETH SEE THEIR CHANCE TO ESCAPE AND DO MAKE IT A FEW FEET*) Wait! Young ladies, you forgot your purse. Sorry for the inconvenience. Have a nice day, but watch out. You young ladies shouldn't be out alone. You never know what might happen to you. (*AMY AND BETH EXIT SHOWING WALLET TO EACH OTHER AND BEGINNING TO GO THROUGH IT*) Now, you scoundrel, you have a date with the police. (*PRIEST MUMBLES SOMETHING AND POINTS AFTER GIRLS*) What's that? Your mask has slipped down and is covering your mouth. No wonder you can't talk. Here, let me help you. (*SUPER CHRISTIAN UNTIES GAG*)

PRIEST: Super Christian. Thank you and bless you.

SUPER CHRISTIAN: Well, you certainly are a holy purse snatcher.

PRIEST: I'm Father Mills.

SUPER CHRISTIAN: (*SHAKING HANDS WITH PRIEST'S TIED HANDS*) Father, you should be ashamed of yourself. Purse snatching, really! Are collections down, or what?

PRIEST: No. No. Those girls just held me up. They're part of a teenage gang terrorizing the city.

SUPER CHRISTIAN: Really?

PRIEST: Really.

SUPER CHRISTIAN: But they were such nice young ladies. And I thought, with the mask and all ... Gosh, I'm sorry.

PRIEST: That's okay. But now that you're here, maybe you'd like to say hello to my young people. You know, tell them some of your adventures.

SUPER CHRISTIAN: I like to save my energies for greater endeavors, like a radio or T.V. show. I reach so many more people that way. Tell the kids to watch me on T.V.

PRIEST: All you have to do is give your witness — the way Jesus has moved in your life. You must have some great stories to tell.

SUPER CHRISTIAN: I do, Father, but I've written a book and I wouldn't want to spoil that for the kids, would I?

PRIEST: But all you have to do is witness.

SUPER CHRISTIAN: Who me, witness? Never!

PRIEST: Since you're writing a book, maybe you'd like to speak to our women's group. There'd probably be a lot of women who'd want to buy your book.

SUPER CHRISTIAN: Actually, I'm making a movie of my life and I wouldn't want to ruin that great movie for anyone.

PRIEST: But, Super Christian ...

SUPER CHRISTIAN: Wait, my X-ray eyes are focusing on a crisis at the city jail. Never mind, you can't see it. See ya. Up, up, and away. (*EXITS*)

ANNOUNCER: Tune in next time for another exciting adventure of Super Christian, when we'll hear Super Christian say ...

SUPER CHRISTIAN: Who, me, witness? Not on your life!

Anger

Theme

Anger is inevitable, but there must be reconciliation or our relationships deteriorate.

Summary

Things are in an uproar at the Pesky home. Rena is trying to find her keys and get Sam, her husband, to paint the bathroom. Rena gets angry.

Playing Time	3 minutes
Setting	The Pesky home
Props	Sam — a shirt with missing buttons
	Rena — a can of interior latex and a paint brush
Costumes	Contemporary, casual
Time	The present
Cast	SAM PESKY
	RENA — his wife
	BILL — their son

SAM: (*ENTERS, CARRYING A SHIRT THAT HE HAS BEEN SEWING BUTTONS ON*) Tiffany? Now where did she go?

RENA: (*ENTERS CARRYING A CAN OF PAINT AND BRUSH WITH A COAT AND TIE DRAPED OVER IT*) Where's Bill? Have you seen him? Bill! (*EXITS*)

SAM: Tiffany! Tiffany! Get in here!

BILL: (*ENTERS*) Yeah?

SAM: Where's your sister?

BILL: How should I know?

SAM: Don't be smart.

BILL: You told me to pull my grades in math and Spanish up, and now you say, "Don't be smart." Make up your mind.

SAM: That's real clever. You know what I mean.

BILL: Yeah, well, I don't know where she is.

SAM: Well, go find her and tell her I want her.

BILL: (*BEGINNING TO EXIT*) Yeah, okay.

RENA: (*ENTERS*) There you are. Where have you been?

BILL: Down in the basement.

RENA: I've been looking all over for you. Where are the car keys?

BILL: (*LEANING AGAINST THE WALL IN A POLICE SEARCH STANCE*) Search me. I didn't take them.

RENA: No one said you did.

BILL: If they were my keys I'll bet I know where they were.

RENA: Don't be smart.

SAM: We covered that territory already.

RENA: What?

SAM: Never mind. It would take too long to explain it to you.

BILL: Can I go now?

RENA: May I.

BILL: You gotta go too?

RENA: Go. Just go. (*BILL EXITS*)

SAM: That kid. I don't know. Everything that comes out of his mouth is some kind of smart answer. Some kind of backtalk. Where do they learn that stuff?

RENA: He learned it from you. You wanted a son just like you. Well, you got him.

SAM: That's cute. That's real cute.

RENA: You've always got some kind of smart comeback for everything I say.

SAM: Ya think so, huh? Well, that's your opinion and it's the wrong opinion.

RENA: (*UNCOVERING THE PAINT CAN AND BRUSH*) Here, I brought you the paint so you can start on the bathroom.

SAM: Will you stop it?

RENA: No, I mean it. You've avoided painting that bathroom long enough. Now get to it.

SAM: I'm tired. I had a rough day.

RENA: I'm tired too. I'm tired of you being the absentee father.

SAM: Absentee father? Been watching too many talk shows, huh? I'm here, aren't I?

RENA: No, you're not. You're on some other planet. A planet where men are men and never pay any attention to their wives.

SAM: Now, you know that's not true. Didn't I get you a nice birthday present?

RENA: A crock pot! You got me a crock pot.

SAM: I was going to get you a Lamborghini but they didn't have any in your favorite colors — fuchsia with puce trim.

RENA: Go paint.

SAM: I want to read the paper and relax a little first.

RENA: Sure, you can read the paper. Put it on the floor in the bathroom and use it to catch the paint splatters.

SAM: Oh, you got a mean streak.

RENA: You've got a lazy streak. You're just like your mother. I never knew anyone as lazy as your mother. The only five-fingered sloth in existence.

SAM: I knew it. Sooner or later you run out of things to yell at me about and then you have to start insulting my parents.

RENA: It's not an insult when it's the truth. Your mother was lazy and your father was a drunkard.

SAM: Oh, so that's the truth, huh? Well, do you want to know the truth about your parents? Huh, do ya?

RENA: I already know the truth about my parents.

SAM: Your parents are ... well, they're perfect.

RENA: That's it?

SAM: Yes, that's it. They were perfect and never let anyone who was less than perfect forget it. Who can live with perfection?

RENA: You have.

SAM: No, I just lived with someone who thought she was perfect.

RENA: I'm closer than you'll ever be.

SAM: That's it. I don't have to listen to this.

RENA: Great. That's great. Go hide in the bathroom and, by the way, paint it while you're crying over your stupid parents.

SAM: Just before I go, I have one question.

RENA: Well?

SAM: Are you angry? (*EXITS*)

Proper 15
John 6:53-59

Son Shine Inn

Theme

Become a part of the body of Christ. Still a difficult statement.

Summary

Bill and Mary Beth are celebrating their anniversary and this new place seems like a nice place to do that. And here comes the waiter who happens to be the owner. It's Jesus, but with a limited menu.

Playing Time	3 minutes
Setting	The Son Shine Inn
Props	Menus, water glasses
Costumes	Contemporary, semi-formal
Time	The present
Cast	BILL
	MARY BETH — his wife
	JESUS

BILL: (*ENTERS WITH MARY BETH AND THEY SIT AT A SMALL TABLE IN A NICE RESTAURANT*) I'm so hungry.

MARY BETH: Me, too. What are you going to have?

BILL: I don't know. I'm ready to celebrate. I know that.

MARY BETH: I thought we might have some champagne.

BILL: Right. Champagne it shall be. Where's the waiter?

247

MARY BETH: I've been looking forward to this all week.

BILL: Me, too. Married two years. (*WITH A TWINKLE IN HIS EYE*) Did you think it would last that long?

MARY BETH: I *knew* it would.

BILL: I love you more now than I ever did.

MARY BETH: I was thinking the same thing.

BILL: You were? (*THEY HOLD HANDS AND GIGGLE*)

JESUS: (*ENTERS. HANDING THEM MENUS*) Good evening, my name is Jesus and I'll be your waiter tonight.

BILL: Jesus?

JESUS: Yes?

BILL: *The* Jesus?

JESUS: The very one. Would you like to begin with cocktails?

(*THE NEXT TWO LINES ARE SPOKEN SIMULTANEOUSLY*)

BILL: No.

MARY BETH: Yes.

BILL: Cocktails? Uh, no. No, thanks. I think we'll just have ...

JESUS: May I suggest the water?

BILL: Yes, water. Great.

JESUS: I'll bring you some living water.

BILL: Yes, living water. That sounds good.

MARY BETH: Yes, I guess so, living water.

JESUS: Well, I'll just get that for you while you look over the menu. (*EXITS*)

MARY BETH: What's "living water"?

BILL: I don't know. But it's got to be better than the city water. Maybe it's distilled or something. (*LOOKING OVER MENU*) What looks good to you?

MARY BETH: I was looking forward to champagne.

BILL: Me too, but you know, this is the *real* Jesus.

MARY BETH: I know. That's what he said. What are you having?

BILL: I don't know. This is kind of a limited menu.

JESUS: (*ENTERS WITH TWO GLASSES OF WATER*) There we go. Two living waters.

BILL: Thank you. Now, about this menu.

JESUS: We serve the very best — true food and true drink.

BILL: If you're really Jesus — the real Jesus ...

JESUS: I am.

BILL: Then what are you doing here, in a restaurant?

JESUS: It's my place.

MARY BETH: Oh, that's nice.

BILL: Nice place.

MARY BETH: (*REFERRING TO MENU*) What exactly is this "Adonai special"?

JESUS: Well, I begin with a fresh loaf of bread.

MARY BETH: Mmm. Fresh bread.

JESUS: Yes, the bread of life.

BILL: Bread of life?

JESUS: I am the bread of life.

BILL: *You* are.

JESUS: Yes. I came down from Heaven. If you partake of the bread you will live forever.

MARY BETH: Came down from ...

JESUS: Heaven.

MARY BETH: Yes.

JESUS: If you want to live ...

BILL: Look, Jesus, we came here ...

JESUS: No one comes here unless the Father draws him.

MARY BETH: I did feel we should come here for our anniversary.

BILL: Did you know we've been married ...

JESUS: Two years, one hour, and, let's see, thirteen minutes.

BILL: You do know.

JESUS: I was there.

MARY BETH: Oh, I don't remember ...

JESUS: Well, would you like the Adonai special?

BILL: I guess so, since it's the only thing on the menu.

MARY BETH: What is it?

JESUS: Lamb.

MARY BETH: And how is it prepared?

JESUS: I prepare it exactly to your taste.

MARY BETH: I like lamb, if it's good.

JESUS: This is perfect. The lamb of God.

BILL: This wouldn't be, by any chance ...

JESUS: It is. I am the lamb of God.

MARY BETH: You are? But I thought you were the bread of life.

JESUS: I am — both.

BILL: Look, Jesus, this is getting to be a bit much.

JESUS: The Father sent me.

BILL: *The* Father?

JESUS: The Father. I live because of the Father. If you partake of the lamb you will live forever.

BILL: Wait just a minute.

JESUS: Does this cause you to stumble?

BILL: Well ...

JESUS: You won't understand everything on the menu. Are you interested?

MARY BETH: I wanted something special for our anniversary.

JESUS: This is special.

BILL: Well, why not.

MARY BETH: Good. Let's have the Lamb of God.

BILL: And begin with the Bread of Life.

JESUS: Now, to begin, may I suggest a drink.

BILL: I'm almost afraid to ask.

JESUS: My blood. It's the only way you can truly abide in me.

BILL: Well, what do you think?

MARY BETH: Oh, yes. After all, it's our anniversary.

JESUS: Good choice. (*EXITS*)

8/27/06

Proper 16
John 6:60-69

Give Up?

Theme:

We give up too easily, especially with things that are spiritual.

Summary:

Two disciples are talking. One of them is thinking about leaving Jesus and the other one, Judas, tries to talk him out of it. But who makes the better choice?

Playing Time	3 1/2 minutes
Setting	The Holy Land
Props	None
Costumes	Disciples of Jesus
Time	The time of Jesus
Cast	MESHULLAM — a disciple
	JUDAS — his friend

JUDAS: (*ENTERS ALONG WITH MESHULLAM*) Settle down.

MESHULLAM: I can't stand it any longer.

JUDAS: What is it? What's bothering you?

MESHULLAM: I'm leaving.

JUDAS: Oh, no, you're not. You told me you would stay with Jesus.

MESHULLAM: I can't accept some of the things he says.

253

JUDAS: Oh, that last thing he said about eating his flesh — is that it?

MESHULLAM: Yes, that's exactly it.

JUDAS: Your trouble is you're trying to understand it.

MESHULLAM: Of course I'm trying to understand it. I'm one of his disciples.

JUDAS: I told you when we started following Jesus not to listen to him.

MESHULLAM: I remember you said that, but I thought you were just joking.

JUDAS: I was not joking. I never joke. This is serious. If Jesus is going to be the Messiah and save our nation from the Romans then it's up to people like us to do it. He's a teacher, a dreamer — you can't expect him to save anyone, can you?

MESHULLAM: He says he will.

JUDAS: Just talk. All people who claim to be the Messiah will talk like that.

MESHULLAM: I believed him at first. But now ...

JUDAS: You started listening to him. That was your first mistake.

MESHULLAM: I used to think his teaching was wonderful. Life-changing.

JUDAS: Listen to me. I'm the one who has the plan. I'm the one who's in charge of the money, aren't I?

MESHULLAM: Yes. You do have all the money.

JUDAS: Well, then I'm the one you should be listening to, right?

MESHULLAM: All right, then, what's your plan?

JUDAS: It's not complicated. All we have to do is use the money we have to pay the people we need. We can pick up some extra money whenever we need it by feeding some information to the officials. They're always ready to pay for information. I know some of the high officials and they said they're sympathetic to our cause. They want to get out from under Rome's rule too.

MESHULLAM: In other words I can just act like a disciple. I don't have to really believe any of the difficult things.

JUDAS: That's right. Jesus himself said we should be as wise as serpents but as innocent as doves.

MESHULLAM: I don't know.

JUDAS: Come on. What do you have to go back to?

MESHULLAM: My family.

JUDAS: Jesus said that if we're not willing to give up our families, then we're not worth following him.

MESHULLAM: For a guy who doesn't listen to him, you quote him a lot.

JUDAS: I listen selectively. I remember what will help our cause.

MESHULLAM: I don't think I can do it.

JUDAS: You can't just quit. Remember what I told you, you're in this until the end.

MESHULLAM: Well, I'm quitting.

JUDAS: Oh, no! You're staying. I need your help.

MESHULLAM: You don't need my help. Your plan seems like a good one, I just want to go home.

JUDAS: Okay, leave then. When Jesus comes into his kingdom I'll be a high official. I'll be the power behind the throne. And where will you be?

MESHULLAM: I'll be home. Good-bye, Judas. (*HE EXITS*)

JUDAS: Loser. (*HE EXITS*)

On A Picnic

Theme:
Speaking about love is always a lot easier than loving.

Summary:
Todd is taking Mandi on a picnic. This sounds like a wonderful way to spend a lovely afternoon, but the path of love is never smooth and Todd is more concerned about his love poem than he is about his love object — Mandi. Todd has a nasty habit of couching everything in spiritual terms and not meaning any of it. Mandi trusts Todd because she mistakenly thinks he cares for her. When she finds out he doesn't, she leaves him.

Playing Time	3 1/2 minutes
Setting	A secluded picnic spot deep in the forest
Time	Turn of the century
Props	A picnic basket and blanket and other picnic things
Costumes	Mandi — a long dress and a long-sleeved, high neck blouse
	Todd — appropriate summer wear for the turn of the century
Cast	MANDI — a lovely young girl
	TODD — her male companion

TODD: (*ENTERS AND CROSSES TO CENTER STAGE CARRYING ONLY HIS LOVE POEM. MANDI AND TODD SPEAK TO EACH OTHER IN LOVEY-DOVEY TONES THROUGHOUT*)
Mandi, my love potion, this is a secluded portion of God's own paradise. A little retreat from the humdrum of everyday life. Our

love will last forever, my darling, and this is the perfect spot for our love tryst.

MANDI: (*ENTERS STRUGGLING WITH A PICNIC BASKET AND OTHER THINGS AND CROSSES TO TODD*) Oh, Toddy, my darling, love, why ever did you choose this place for our picnic? (*DROPPING SOME OF THE MANY THINGS SHE IS CARRYING*) Toddy, love dumpling, may I be so bold as to remind you that we have been walking for an hour now in God's paradise?

TODD: Certainly, heart of my heart, you may so remind me.

MANDI: Then, I do so remind you, my sweet-faced pumpkin. May I also remind you that my feet are sore?

TODD: And could I please bring to your attention, delight of my eyes, that you have dropped some of the things that you were carrying?

MANDI: Yes, of course you could bring such a catastrophe to my attention, because you are the conqueror of my heart, you are my Atilla the honey. (*TWEAKING HIM UNDER THE CHIN*)

TODD: (*PICKING UP THE DROPPED THINGS AND PLACING THEM BACK IN MANDI'S ARMS*) Here, let me be of assistance to you, my flower of exquisite beauty, my daisy of delightfulness.

MANDI: Thank you so very much. You are the ever-helpful one. You are the treasure at the end of my rainbow of desire. (*SHE BUMPS INTO TODD*)

TODD: And now, dreadnaught of delectableness, we can continue our journey. And when we reach our destination I will tell you of my great love by means of a love poem that I have created which was inspired by God.

MANDI: Toddy, my sweet pea, could we stop in this lovely glen and partake of the food which we have been carrying for a mile or more?

TODD: Yes, of course, if you so wish, my passion flower. It is in this place that I will recite my love poem inspired by the Creator of this paradise.

MANDI: I do so wish to stop here, my precious jewel, the sapphire of my desire. (*RELEASING HER LOAD*) Whew!

TODD: Then we will disencumber ourselves of this paraphernalia and share each with the other that which we have brought, my dearest, delightsome delfinium.

MANDI: (*SHE SITS AND REMOVES HER SHOES ALTHOUGH TODD DOES NOT NOTICE BECAUSE HE IS INTERESTED IN HIS POEM*) I think that this is a most enchanting glade. We shall enjoy each other and our repast, my affecionate confectionary, my chocolate-covered love-berry.

TODD: Mandi, you are the cucumber of my contentment, but may I suggest, my engaging expression of excitement, that we must not sit.

MANDI: (*SHE STANDS AND REFRESHES HER FEET BY WALKING BAREFOOTED*) You may so suggest, my most excellent, extravagant, exceedingly exquisite exchequer of my heart's treasure.

TODD: Then I do so suggest, my entrancing enchantress.

MANDI: I know you are ever-wise, my Solomon of snuggledom, but may I inquire why it is that we may not sit?

TODD: Of course, you may so inquire, my luscious, luxuriant lullaby of loveliness.

MANDI: Then I do so inquire, my tantalizing tweedle-tweaker.

TODD: My winsomeness, we should stand in the presence of such lovely natural beauty.

MANDI: Here in this delightful glen, my sweet feet?

TODD: Yes, my entrancing seductress.

MANDI: But why should we not sit? Do I hear you correctly, my alluring one?

TODD: You do indeed hear correctly, oh rapturous, rhapsodic romancer. We must not sit because there might, perchance, be poison ivy growing here.

MANDI: Oh, no! (*SHE CROSSES RIGHT AND PUTS HER SHOES ON AS BEST SHE CAN WITHOUT SITTING*) Can you identify poison ivy, my beloved blinker wink?

TODD: Why, no, I cannot, my questioning cutie.

MANDI: Am I to understand that we transported this entire collection of picnic paraphernalia a mile or so, all the fried chicken and potato salad that I prepared with my own two willing hands, and we are to partake of it standing all the while, my love cruncher?

TODD: Alas, it must be so, my irresistible, impassioned one.

MANDI: Allow me to inform you, my infatuated paramour, in a manner of speaking, I will not stand for it. (*MANDI BEGINS TO EXIT*)

TODD: But Mandi, my petulant pearl of great price, who will help me carry these many things back?

MANDI: (*EXITING*) May I suggest, my charming circus of circumstance, that you make two trips, and be advised that I will not be your companion on either one of them. (*TWEAKING HIS CHEEK*)

TODD: I thought God's paradise would be more hospitable. Paradise could be attained in this world if only everyone were more like me. Ah, well, I never liked her much anyway. (*TEARING UP HIS LOVE POEM. GATHERING UP EVERYTHING AND EXITING*)

All Things Well

Theme:
The kingdom of God and the new life it brings to individuals is certainly something to tell the entire world.

Summary:
Jesus is healing people and that is good news. Although Jesus tells them not to tell anyone, the thrilling news is too good to keep to themselves.

Playing Time	2 minutes
Setting	Your church
Props	None
Costumes	Rapper
Time	Now
Cast	RAPPER

RAPPER: (*ENTERS*) Who was that man,
That man who heals?
What does he think he's doing?
Who does he think he is?
A whiz?
Disrupting,
Interrupting the natural order.
The way things are — the border,
Which you cannot cross.
Destructive, to heal a man who cannot hear and doesn't speak,
Who isn't talkative.
To make him well,
To make him normal.

I cannot tell you,
It was not formal.
Didn't do it at a meeting.
A casual greeting,
And then the man is leading
Others to Him.
Entreating,
Those who are needing
Someone who can be feeding
Them the kingdom news.
He only laid on hands,
And stuck his fingers in the deaf man's ears,
And years
Of isolation and pain
Did not remain.
The reign
Of God is here.
Jesus is walking near.
Do not fear.
It is clear.
He wants to help us.
He cares for all.
He'll tear down the wall
That surrounds us all.
He's found our hurt and healed it.
He revealed it,
Repealed the pain, the isolation.
Jesus our Lord, God of all creation.
He doesn't ration
His love.
He gives it in full measure.
He is our treasure.
Our Lord and master.
And faster
Than a word
He heals those who cannot speak or hear a sound.
He found us when we were lost.

And paid the cost
To free us from sin,
So we can win
Over death and disease.
So, please
Give your heart
To our Savior.
Make a start.
A new way is waiting.
The path you're anticipating
Is free for the taking.
Then with Jesus the bread you'll be breaking.
Where your heart has been aching,
Your spirit will be waking
To new joys.
Making a joyful noise.
And you can say what all the reborns tell,
That he does all things well.
(*HE EXITS*)

Lust

Theme

The evil one has ways of ruining our lives. If we don't have Jesus — we don't have hope. If we don't believe in Jesus all things are not possible.

Summary

Things are calming down at the Pesky home, or so they think. Rena has taken care of sewing the buttons on Sam's shirt and he has finally painted the bathroom, but Bill, their son, has been looking at pornography.

Playing Time	3 minutes
Setting	The Pesky home
Props	Sam — an empty can of interior latex and a paint brush
	Rena — a shirt with buttons sewn on, covering a pornographic magazine and business card
Costumes	Contemporary, casual
Time	The present
Cast	SAM PESKY
	RENA — his wife
	BILL — their son

SAM: (*ENTERS CARRYING AN EMPTY CAN OF PAINT AND BRUSH*) Rena! I got the bathroom painted.

RENA: (*ENTERS, CARRYING A SHIRT THAT SHE HAS BEEN SEWING BUTTONS ON WHICH IS COVERING A PORNO-GRAPHIC MAGAZINE*) That's great, Sam. Here's your shirt. I sewed the buttons on.

SAM: Can you beat that. We seem to be getting our act together. I painted the bathroom and you sewed the buttons on my shirt. Our marriage works.

RENA: Well, maybe. Look at this. (*HANDING HIM THE POR-NOGRAPHIC MAGAZINE*)

SAM: I've been looking all over for that issue. Where did you find it?

RENA: Down in the basement.

SAM: Where?

RENA: You know that space behind the furnace back by the back wall, well, your son has a clubhouse down there.

SAM: And that's where you found this?

RENA: Right. You've got to say something to him.

SAM: (*FLIPPING THROUGH MAGAZINE*) Now, wait a minute. What's wrong with this stuff? He has to learn about it sometime.

RENA: I knew that's what you'd say.

SAM: What do you mean? That's what you used to say. We used to look at better stuff than this — videos.

RENA: I know, and I've been thinking about that.

SAM: And?

266

RENA: Well. I just think you better stop Bill before it's too late.

BILL: He's old enough. Don't be such an old granny.

RENA: Stop it, Sam. Don't give me any more backtalk about it.

SAM: Whoa. What's this? You got awful testy all of a sudden.

RENA: Just do something about Bill, will you?

SAM: Why should I?

RENA: Because I think it's important. I'm worried about him.

BILL: You're worried about your son's natural urges?

RENA: I just don't want him to grow up to be like you.

SAM: And what's wrong with me?

RENA: You don't want to know.

SAM: I want to know what you think is wrong with me.

RENA: Just take care of Bill, will you?

SAM: No, I won't.

RENA: Please, Sam. Just do it and leave me alone.

SAM: I'm not moving from this spot until you tell me what it is that's bugging you.

RENA: Okay. It's more than just Bill looking at that magazine. A whole lot more. It's you too.

SAM: You're kidding, right?

RENA: No, I'm not kidding. I've just begun to realize that the reason you don't pay any attention to me any more is because of those magazines.

SAM: What?

RENA: It's true, isn't it?

SAM: No, it is not true.

RENA: You are in love with those airbrushed perfect bodies and you don't have time for me any more.

SAM: That's nonsense.

RENA: Then why haven't you touched me in the past six months?

SAM: You know the long hours I work.

RENA: I know I found this in your pants pocket. (*PRODUCING A BUSINESS CARD AND HANDING IT TO HIM*)

SAM: What's this?

RENA: It's a business card from a massage parlor in Washington, D.C.

SAM: I ...

RENA: What's it going to be next? Will you be picking up some whore next? Wait a minute. How do I know you haven't done that already? I don't, do I?
You've got a problem, Sam. It's not innocently looking at some girlie magazines any more. You've got a problem and you've infected this entire family with it. You've stopped caring about me and now you want to make Bill into someone just like you. Where will it end? Next you'll be lusting after your own daughter. (*SHE EXITS RUNNING AND CRYING*)

Proper 20
Mark 9:30-37

Greatness

Theme

The kingdom of God is different than any other. To be first in the kingdom you must be servant of all.

Summary

Peter, James, and John want to be great and they are arguing about their achievements. Jesus sets them straight.

Playing Time	3 minutes
Setting	The Holy Land
Props	A small black book
Costumes	Peasant, first century
Time	The time of Christ
Cast	PETER
	JAMES
	JOHN
	JESUS

JAMES: (*ENTERS CARRYING A SMALL BLACK BOOK*) I've got the list right here. You'll see.

PETER: (*ENTERS*) Throw that list away. His kingdom is above such things.

JOHN: (*ENTERS*) I should say it is. His kingdom is a kingdom of faith. I have that faith, therefore I shall rule with him.

269

JAMES: I think you shall, too. And I know I will. Let me read this list to you. It's an account I have kept since we have been together.

PETER: Aren't you the one to keep accounts. You mark down everything. I don't hold with your list — your account.

JAMES: That's because you know you'll come up short. I'll tell you the truth. John, here is the one who looks like he's going to rule with the Master.

JOHN: You see. I told you so.

PETER: Nonsense. (*PUSHING JOHN OUT OF THE WAY, GRABBING BOOK FROM JAMES*)

JAMES: Hey!

JOHN: Let him alone. The big dummy. Look how unspiritual you are. The Master doesn't want a big oaf like you ruling in his kingdom. Mother assured James and me that we would both rule with the Master when he comes into his kingdom.

PETER: (*READING FROM BOOK*) This is stupid. "John was closest to Jesus when we were on that mountain and he was changed." Are you serious? I'm the only one who said anything. You two were too dumb.

JOHN: Watch your mouth. Read on.

PETER: "Peter sticks his foot in his mouth again." I'm tearing this out of here.

JAMES: You just keep your big nose out of my business.

PETER: "Who passed out the most bread and fish when feeding the five thousand: John — three thousand, two hundred and thirty-one pieces of bread, James — two thousand, eight hundred and seventeen pieces of fish, Peter — one thousand twenty-eight."

JOHN: I guess that tells the tale, eh, Peter?

PETER: Well, I didn't know we were in a contest. I was trying to be kind to people.

JOHN: The Master wants rulers in his kingdom who can do miracles, be kind to people, and get the job done fast and efficiently. Some of us do that better than others, that's all. I'm going to tell you my secret. I pray a lot. That's why I have so much faith. Look it up in the book how many demons I cast out when we were out on our own.

PETER: I'm tired of reading about your spiritual exploits in this dumb book. I don't care. The Master will use me because I am a good friend of his.

JAMES: That's ridiculous. A good friend? What good is that?

JESUS: (*ENTERS*) What were you discussing on the way here? (*PICKING UP A SMALL CHILD AND HOLDING HER*) Gather around. If any of you want to be first you must be servant of all. Here, look at this child. Whoever receives one little child like this in my name is receiving me, and not only me, but God the Father.

Hell!

Theme

Hell is real. Jesus taught about it. Stay away from it and tell your friends, too.

Summary

During a talk show the host is asking the question: "What is your view of hell?" He gets some good information from the Bible and then experiences it himself.

Playing Time	6 minutes
Setting	A television talk show
Props	Microphone
Costumes	Contemporary
Time	The time of truth
Cast	HOST
	BILL
	JOHN
	PAM
	WILLOW
	ANGEL I
	ANGEL II

(TWO ANGELS ENTER AND STAND ON EITHER SIDE OF THE PLATFORM)

HOST: *(ENTERS AND MOVES THROUGH THE AUDIENCE)*
Our question today is: "What is your view of hell?" What about you? What is your view of hell?

JOHN: (*STANDS*) I see hell as a place of final punishment for those who reject Jesus.

HOST: You think hell is an actual place, then.

JOHN: Yes, of course. The Bible teaches that it is.

HOST: Where is that in the Bible, do you know?

JOHN: No, I don't know exactly.

PAM: I know a reference.

HOST: Wait until I get there with the microphone. (*CROSSES TO PAM*) Now, then, you say you know of a reference in the Bible referring to hell?

PAM: It says in the story of the Rich Man and Lazarus that it is a place of torment.

HOST: This is interesting. You say it's an actual place, and not only a place but a place of torment.

PAM: Right. That story is in Luke 16.

HOST: Thank you. People can look that up on their own, but for now let's continue with our question for the day: "What is your view of hell?" How about you?

WILLOW: (*STANDS*) In the Bible study I attend our teacher said there are quite a few different words that are translated "hell" in the Bible.

HOST: Now, this will help. What were those different words?

PAM: Pardon me.

HOST: Yes?

PAM: (*SPEAKING TO WILLOW*) Don't you remember, our teacher said there were four words that are translated "hell."

WILLOW: I didn't remember how many.

HOST: Do you remember the words?

PAM: I wrote them down. Here they are: *Tartaraho* (2 Peter 2:4) — a Greek word that refers to a place meant for sinning angels. *Ge-enna* (Mark 9:48) — another Greek word that represents a Hebrew word with the concept of unquenchable fire and an undying worm.

HOST: That's very graphic.

WILLOW: The Bible is like that sometimes.

HOST: And you said there were two more words translated "hell."

PAM: Yes, another Greek word, *hades,* which means the underworld or the region of the departed. An intermediate place between death and future resurrection.

HOST: And the other word?

PAM: *Sheol,* a Hebrew word meaning about the same as *hades.* It is a place where the dead, both bad and good, dwell together.

HOST: Then the Bible teaches that the good and bad dwell together after death.

BILL: No, no. That's not right.

HOST: Oh, so you disagree?

BILL: Jesus changed things. Jesus conquered death by coming back to life after he was dead. And while he was dead he entered the realm of hades and freed the righteous dead that were there. (1 Peter 3:18-20; Ephesians 4:8-10)

HOST: So, you're saying that Jesus changed what happens to the dead?

BILL: He sure did. Now, when the righteous die they go directly to be with Jesus. (2 Corinthians 5:8)

HOST: And what about the others, those who reject Jesus?

BILL: They still go to hades where they are tormented and where they await their judgment. (Revelation 20:11-15)

HOST: So, you're saying that the unrighteous dead go through torment during the waiting period and then they are condemned to eternal torment, right?

BILL: Not me. That's what the Bible says.

HOST: Now, wait a minute. That doesn't sound like a loving God to me. How can you reconcile this God of judgment with a God of love?

BILL: It's all God's personality. God's love is part of God. So is God's judgment.

HOST: How can that be?

BILL: God is holy, right?

HOST: That's what I've been told.

BILL: God is holy and therefore cannot be associated with unholiness. The judgment is actually part of the holiness. Those who reject Jesus actually place themselves in a position that is unholy and therefore they have chosen their own future — judgment.

HOST: You're getting this from the Bible, right?

BILL: That's right.

HOST: Well, I don't happen to believe in the Bible.

BILL: But what if the Bible is true? What will you do then?

ANGEL I: He doesn't understand.

ANGEL II: No. Show him death and hell.

(*HOST FALLS DEAD ON THE FLOOR*)

PAM: What in the world?

BILL: He's dead!

WILLOW: He just keeled over.

(*ANGEL I, ALONG WITH ANGEL II, TAKE HOST BY THE ARMS AND LIFT HIM UP*)

HOST: What's happening? Where am I going?

ANGEL II: You'll recognize it when you get there.

HOST: Oh, no! I do recognize it. This is hell! Aargh! The worm ...

ANGEL II: You decided to come here.

HOST: I didn't decide anything. No, no, not that! No, no, get away from me. Aargh!

ANGEL I: You made a decision. Not deciding is a decision. *(ANGEL I AND ANGEL II BEGIN TO EXIT)*

HOST: No, you can't leave me here. Please come back. It's so black. I can't see a thing. It's so lonely. Don't leave me, please. Aaiee! *(HOST SHAKES HIS HEAD AS IF ALL THIS WAS A BAD DREAM)*

BILL: I said, what if the Bible is true? What will you do then?

HOST: Wow. Sorry. I just had a weird thought.

BILL: Oh, yeah, what was that?

HOST: Oh, nothing, never mind.

BILL: Well, what do you think about what the Bible says about hell?

HOST: I don't believe a word of it. Not a word. *(EXITING)* I'll think about it some more.

ANGEL I: Tiresome, aren't they?

ANGEL II: He may not have as long as he thinks.

Divorce

Theme
Divorce is a decision, just as love is a decision.

Summary
A husband and wife are talking about the wife's decision to leave her husband for another man. The husband has also made a decision — to love his wife and forgive her.

Playing Time	3 minutes
Setting	At home
Props	None
Costumes	Contemporary
Time	Now
Cast	HUSBAND
	WIFE

(HUSBAND AND WIFE ARE TALKING AS THEY ENTER)

WIFE: Yes. Yes!

HUSBAND: No. No!

WIFE: Oh, yes, you will.

HUSBAND: Oh, no, I won't.

WIFE: You will, because I don't love you.

HUSBAND: I still won't give you a divorce.

WIFE: Yes, you will. I have friends that will testify for me in court.

HUSBAND: You won't ever get to court, because I'm not going to file for divorce and you won't.

WIFE: And why won't I file for divorce?

HUSBAND: You just won't.

WIFE: I'll make you so miserable you'll be glad to divorce me.

HUSBAND: Impossible. You can't make things so miserable that I would ever divorce you.

WIFE: We'll see.

HUSBAND: Never.

WIFE: But I love Bob.

HUSBAND: You could love me again.

WIFE: Never. Not ever again. I doubt if I ever loved you at all.

HUSBAND: You're confused.

WIFE: I guess I know my own mind.

HUSBAND: You're confused. If you'd just be willing to get some counseling ...

WIFE: We tried that, remember?

HUSBAND: You weren't willing to try.

WIFE: I tried.

HUSBAND: You walked out.

WIFE: It was useless.

HUSBAND: I was willing to change, why weren't you?

WIFE: Change? Listen, I've changed. I've matured. You're the one who needs to mature.

HUSBAND: Me?

WIFE: You're about to tell me how mature you are, right?

HUSBAND: Well, no, not really, I'm not, but I'm willing to work on it. If you'd just be ...

WIFE: Good. Great. Work on it. But work on it alone.

HUSBAND: Alone? Why? Why can't we work on it together?

WIFE: I need my freedom.

HUSBAND: But you won't be free. You'll be the slave of this other man.

WIFE: Bob. I won't be his slave. He makes me happy. I haven't been happy for fourteen years.

HUSBAND: You can't say that.

WIFE: It's true. All I've ever had with you is responsibility. Loads of responsibilities. And I'm sick and tired of it. I tell you I want my freedom. I'm leaving. I don't care if you divorce me or not. I'm leaving. You'll find someone else.

HUSBAND: I found you a long time ago and I'll be ...

WIFE: Waiting? Is that what you were going to say? You'll be waiting? You'll wait until my little fling is over and you'll be there waiting for the wayward wife, right?

HUSBAND: That's about right.

WIFE: Then you're going to get awfully old waiting. I'm leaving and I'm not coming back — ever.

HUSBAND: Oh, you'll be back.

WIFE: Well, then, grow old waiting. I don't care.

HUSBAND: Well, I do. I do care. And I'll be here waiting for you.

WIFE: That's the most ridiculous thing I've ever heard. You'll find someone else. You'll see.

HUSBAND: I won't.

WIFE: How can you be so sure?

HUSBAND: I'm sure.

WIFE: You'll be lonely and the right person will come along and ...

HUSBAND: That will never happen.

WIFE: And why not?

HUSBAND: It's very simple. I love you and I already told you — I'll wait for you.

WIFE: No matter how long I might be gone?

HUSBAND: I'll be here ready to show you I love you. Can Bob give you that?

WIFE: Bob loves me.

HUSBAND: Not with the same degree of love that I have.

WIFE: Of course he does.

HUSBAND: He can't.

WIFE: Bob loves me. I'm completely happy with Bob.

HUSBAND: You're just in love with no responsibility. But you won't be able to escape it. How will Bob's love hold up to everyday problems and stresses?

WIFE: We'll have each other. Why don't you want me to be happy?

HUSBAND: Believe me, that's all I think about.

WIFE: If you do then you'd give me a divorce.

HUSBAND: Never.

WIFE: Our love will be finished.

HUSBAND: Never.

WIFE: It's finished now.

HUSBAND: Not as long as I love you.

WIFE: But how can you love me? You don't know all the terrible things I've done.

HUSBAND: I don't want to know.

WIFE: I want to tell you.

HUSBAND: I want to tell you something first.

WIFE: What?

HUSBAND: I forgive you.

WIFE: You don't know all the things.

HUSBAND: I don't have to know anything you've done to forgive you.

WIFE: If you knew the things I've done ... If you knew, you wouldn't forgive.

HUSBAND: It doesn't make a bit of difference. I forgive you.

WIFE: (*CRYING*) No. No.

HUSBAND: (*HOLDING HER*) Yes. Yes.

WIFE: You can't forgive.

HUSBAND: I can and I do. I forgive you.

WIFE: How can you? How?

HUSBAND: I already told you. I decided to forgive.

WIFE: You decided...?

HUSBAND: I decided to forgive you, just as I decided to love you.

10/15/06

Success

Theme

What is success? Can it be bought or achieved or is it found in the security of God's will?

Summary

Bryan is a young man who is sure he has it all. He is young and has a good job. His future is guaranteed. He is successful at all he does so, of course, he thinks he can nail down this "spiritual thing." He gets his chance when he hears Jesus speak and then talks with him afterward. Jesus shows him the right path, but will Bryan take it?

Playing Time	4 minutes
Setting	By the coffee machine in a big corporation
Props	Two coffee cups
Costumes	Street clothes except for Jesus, who might wear a traditional robe
Time	Now
Cast	BRYAN — a wealthy young man who has made it by knowing the answers and putting them into practice
	JESUS

(JESUS ENTERS CARRYING A COFFEE CUP)

BRYAN: *(ENTERS, CARRYING A COFFEE CUP AND HURRYING TO CATCH JESUS)* Oh, Jesus, your speech was really impressive. I can learn a lot from guys like you, like eternal life and how to get it, and that sort of thing. You're a good teacher.

JESUS: Why do you call me good? Only God is good.

BRYAN: Now wait a minute. You are a good teacher.

JESUS: Thank you. Are you a good student?

BRYAN: You bet I am. I'm a vice president of a Fortune 500 corporation. I apply what I learn.

JESUS: But you haven't learned anything about goodness.

BRYAN: About goodness? Like what? Teach me.

JESUS: You think a person can be good.

BRYAN: Well, of course I do. I've been good all my life.

JESUS: Have you?

BRYAN: You bet I have. I'm successful. I've followed the rules. I just want to nail down this spiritual thing.

JESUS: You've broken a few rules.

BRYAN: A few, maybe. Not very many. Not as many as some others.

JESUS: Hmm.

BRYAN: Now wait a minute. I wanted to talk about eternal life. Not goodness.

JESUS: You don't understand about goodness. You won't understand about eternal life.

BRYAN: Okay. I admit you could teach me something. So, go ahead, teach.

JESUS: You cannot earn goodness.

BRYAN: That's deep. No one can earn goodness? I can't be good by trying to be good? Is that what you're saying?

JESUS: That's it.

BRYAN: But how can that be? I've always been told to "be good." How could people tell me to do that if it wasn't possible?

JESUS: Most people are teaching what they don't know.

BRYAN: Oh.

JESUS: Some people are trying to be good.

BRYAN: Uh-huh. But what you're saying is that a person cannot be good by trying to be good.

JESUS: You've said it. Do you understand what you said?

BRYAN: No.

JESUS: Goodness cannot be attained by human achievement.

BRYAN: Then how can it be attained?

JESUS: Who is good?

BRYAN: You said God alone is good.

JESUS: Then doesn't it make sense that God alone can make people good?

BRYAN: Yes, it does make sense. But how does God do it?

JESUS: God won't make you good until you let him.

BRYAN: How do I let God make me good?

JESUS: How bad do you want it?

BRYAN: With all my life.

JESUS: That's exactly what it will cost.

BRYAN: My life!

JESUS: Yes. You sacrifice your life for God. He gives you goodness.

BRYAN: You make it sound easy.

JESUS: Believe me, it isn't. I know.

BRYAN: If you can do it, I can do it.

JESUS: That's right. That's how you do it. I'll help you.

BRYAN: I don't know.

JESUS: It's worth it.

BRYAN: Yes, I suppose it is.

JESUS: Well?

BRYAN: Everything. That's a lot to give up.

JESUS: To be good? That's a lot to have.

BRYAN: I don't know.

JESUS: Your choice.

BRYAN: Well, I'll think about it. (*HE EXITS*)

JESUS: Oh, yes, you'll think about it. All the time, you'll think about it.

Power

Theme:

The power that is eternal is available to Christians in any and all situations. It is the power of serving.

Summary:

Tim has just been promoted and is enthusiastic about the new opportunity. His superior, Carl, is trying to help him become a better leader by teaching him to be a servant, but Tim has some reservations.

Playing Time	5 minutes
Setting	Tim and Carl's business office
Props	None
Costumes	Business
Time	The present
Cast	TIM — a businessman
	CARL — his superior

CARL: (*ENTERS ALONG WITH TIM*) So, how's it working out?

TIM: With the new division? Not bad.

CARL: I thought it might.

TIM: I appreciate the promotion.

CARL: Well, I think I picked the right person for the job.

TIM: Thanks. I like the challenge. My people seem to be doing well. Production is up seven percent.

CARL: I've got some ideas that will help you.

TIM: I'm open to anything that will help me be more effective.

CARL: I hoped you would say that.

TIM: Let's hear those ideas.

CARL: Well, to begin with, I want you to serve your people.

TIM: Serve?

CARL: Yes, I want you to be their servant.

TIM: Whoa! What are you talking about — serving?

CARL: You're supposed to be their servant.

TIM: You're joking.

CARL: I'm not joking. I'm serious.

TIM: Come on, Carl, what are you talking about?

CARL: I mean serve your people. Be there to help them.

TIM: I'm there to see that they do their work.

CARL: True enough, you are, but you're also in the position to help them.

TIM: Help them, how? I thought they were being helped by getting their paycheck and by their benefit package.

CARL: No. That's what they work for. They earn that.

TIM: What else is there to helping them? I can't hold their hands and guide them through life.

CARL: No, that's God's job, but you're God's man in this job. Therefore that means you have to serve the people you're responsible for.

TIM: You're going to have to prove that to me.

CARL: All right. I've heard you say you want to succeed.

TIM: I do. I'll do anything it takes to succeed at this job.

CARL: Well, your attitude is right, that's for sure.

TIM: I try.

CARL: I've seen that in you. But you don't have a servant heart.

TIM: No, I guess I don't. I missed that lesson in leadership training.

CARL: That's because you've only had the company training.

TIM: And what kind of training have you had?

CARL: I've had the same company training you had, but I also went to "Servant Training."

TIM: Where'd you go for that?

CARL: To my Bible.

TIM: Oh.

CARL: Don't give me that look.

TIM: It's just that I don't think the Bible is appropriate right now. Not on the job. What is appropriate is that I do my job and increase production and profits and keep injuries to a minimum and do what I know how to do.

CARL: All the things you've been trained to do.

TIM: Of course. You wouldn't have promoted me if you didn't think I could produce.

CARL: True enough, but I also hoped you would be willing to learn.

TIM: I am.

CARL: But not from the Bible.

TIM: You don't expect me to have a Bible study at work, do you?

CARL: No, I don't.

TIM: Well, what then? How am I supposed to be their servant?

CARL: Listen to them.

TIM: We have a suggestion box.

CARL: How many suggestions do you get?

TIM: A few.

CARL: I know. Remember, I used to have your job. I know that it takes time to write out a suggestion and drop it in the box. How many do you answer?

TIM: We use a few.

CARL: You use a few of the few. There's a better way. By listening to your workers. In that way they get the chance to explain it and you can watch their gestures and facial expressions.

TIM: Their non-verbals.

CARL: Oh, you know about that.

TIM: Sure. It's easier to talk to someone in person than it is on the phone.

CARL: Or trying to communicate through the suggestion box.

TIM: Listening. Right. I can do that. Is that it?

CARL: That's part of it.

TIM: What else?

CARL: This is the tough part. Give them whatever they need to get their job done.

TIM: What's tough about that? We do that. Our company is very innovative.

CARL: It is. But as you're listening to the ideas of your workers you have to evaluate those ideas and put those that are worthy into practice. Then you have to give them everything they need to see their idea come into being.

TIM: Sort of like a doctor helping a mother birth a child.

CARL: Yes. Sort of. If they need it — you get it for them.

TIM: That's easy enough.

CARL: Well, it's sure easier to talk about than it is to do.

TIM: You did that for me when you were my boss.

CARL: And how did it work?

TIM: Great. You helped me reach my full potential.

CARL: In that particular job. You haven't reached your full potential yet.

TIM: I hope not.

CARL: I'm always here to serve you.

TIM: Hey, that's right. You are, aren't you?

CARL: Right. Just like you have to be for your workers.

TIM: I see what you mean. I can do that. Maybe production will be up even further.

CARL: Probably. Let's hope so.

10/29/06

Blind No More

Theme:

Faith takes some doing on the part of the person.

Summary:

Bartimaeus tells his story. He was healed by Jesus and he is anxious to spread the good news about Jesus. A monologue.

Playing Time	5 minutes
Setting	Your church
Props	None
Costumes	First century, beggar
Time	The present
Cast	BARTIMAEUS

BARTIMAEUS: (*ENTERS*) So, what do you think? About me, I mean? What do you think?

Oh, wait a minute. They told me you would be people from Jericho. You're not from Jericho, are you? Well, that's the problem then. You don't know me. That explains why you didn't recognize me. I'm Bartimaeus. I used to be called blind Bartimaeus. Now I'm just known as Bartimaeus.

People who know me are shocked to see that I'm not blind anymore. Then I get to tell them about Jesus. It's a great way to get the opportunity to talk to people about the Savior.

So that's what I'm going to do here, now. I'm going to tell you about Jesus. Don't tell me you've heard it all. You haven't. With Jesus there's always something new.

I was going to tell you my story anyway. I can't stop talking about it. Believe me, you'd be the same way.

I was a beggar. I always sat by Jericho's western gate alongside the road. I had been there from sunup to sundown every day except the Sabbath since I was three years old. I've been blind since I was three. It was an accident. Anyway, there I was in my usual spot when Jesus came along.

I want to tell you something, it wasn't just Jesus. He had a regular parade going there. People were all over the place. You see, Jesus was going up to Jerusalem and that meant he was going to go head to head with the temple authorities there. People always like a good fight and they figured that Jesus was enough of a prophet to give them a good fight.

I yelled out, "Jesus, Son of David, have mercy on me!" I mean I yelled, I screamed. Otherwise I wouldn't have been heard above all that crowd noise.

Some people tried to hush me up, but here was my only chance. I knew Jesus could heal my blind eyes. I had heard all the stories. He had healed a lot of people. Why not me?

You know it's a strange thing, but the longer a person is sick or has some problem like I did, well, it's like people just accept you as you are and expect you to stay that way. Well, I didn't. I knew Jesus could heal me. So, I yelled louder. "Jesus, Son of David, have mercy on me!"

You see, I went to synagogue every Sabbath and so I knew my scriptures, that's why I called Jesus "Son of David." He was in the royal line, you know. You didn't know that? Well, a lot of people didn't know that. But I knew. I studied the scriptures. Here was Jesus, the Promised One, the Messiah, my only hope.

Calling him "Son of David" got his attention because he'd never been called that before — never. So he listened.

Jesus called me to him and one of the disciples came over to me and said, "Take courage, arise! He is calling for you." Good words. I'm telling you they were encouraging words.

It took courage just to get up. But I did. I jumped up. I did and it has changed my life. I got up and threw off my cloak. I threw it away because that was the way I caught the coins thrown my way. I was never going back to being a beggar again. Jesus was calling me. I was about to be healed.

I don't know if you know what begging does for a person's soul. It kills something in you. You become a whining, cheap imitation of a human being. I was that person. And I wasn't going back — ever.

I walked straight to Jesus. All my life others had led me to my begging place alongside the road, but now I walked without any help. I was determined. Jesus had called me. I had the faith to walk to him.

I went to Jesus and he asked me, "What do you want me to do for you?" Now, you may think that's a strange question, but it's honest and I answered it honestly.

I had been a beggar as long as I could remember, but now I wasn't begging, I was answering in faith, "Teacher, I want to regain my sight." You know what? I could have asked for anything. Here he was, the son of God, asking me what I wanted. I wanted my sight again. I wanted to see things like I had before. To be a man who could work and support a family. I wanted to use my talents for the Lord, Jesus. I wanted my sight back.

Jesus said, "Go your way, your faith has made you well." That was what I wanted to hear. But I didn't go my way. I went his way. I followed him. I still do.

Who here can say the same? Follow him in faith as I did. That's all you have to do. Jesus will take care of you. Follow him.

Right Next Door

Theme

All too often the evil we see in another is the evil that is within ourselves. The beatitudes are at their core a plea for a pure heart. This cannot be attained by striving but by the ministry of the Holy Spirit. Then we can be trustworthy and forgiving.

Summary

Stan and his wife Chloe are in the midst of a fight that has lasted all week. Stan is accusing Chloe of flirting with a neighbor, but it is Stan who has been having an affair with the neighbor's wife — right next door.

Playing Time	3 1/2 minutes
Setting	Modern day — Stan and Chloe's home
Props	Paper for Stan
Costumes	Modern
Time	The present
Cast	STAN — a worldly man
	CHLOE — his wife

CHLOE: *(ENTERS ALONG WITH STAN. STAN IS READING THE PAPER)* How long?

STAN: How long what?

CHLOE: You know what.

STAN: Leave me alone.

CHLOE: You haven't talked to me since Friday.

STAN: I'm talking to you now.

CHLOE: You know what I mean. Talk to me!

STAN: I'm busy.

CHLOE: I can't stand it.

STAN: Leave me alone.

CHLOE: Talk to me!

STAN: No!

CHLOE: (*SNATCHING THE PAPER FROM HIS HANDS*) You will talk to me!

STAN: (*CLENCHING HIS FIST AND DRAWING IT BACK*) Don't make me hit you!

CHLOE: (*DEFIANTLY, BUT STAYING OUT OF HIS REACH*) What's new, huh, Stan? What's new? Go ahead, hit me. Hit me. If you hit me at least I know you're relating to me. Go ahead. I'm almost used to it. Hit me!

STAN: Get outta here.

CHLOE: I will not! We're going to talk.

STAN: Who cares about you?

CHLOE: What is it? What is it, Stan? What's going on?

STAN: You know.

CHLOE: I was only talking to him. I told you that. Just talking. And you blew it up into this big thing.

STAN: You were talking to him for an awfully long time.

CHLOE: Stan, I told you. It was only talk. We were just making small talk.

STAN: Small talk about what?

CHLOE: Just about his work and stuff. I don't know.

STAN: I don't want you talking to him anymore.

CHLOE: He's our neighbor, our next-door neighbor. How can I not talk to him?

STAN: Just don't. That's all.

CHLOE: I've got to talk to him once in a while. He's our next-door neighbor. Be reasonable.

STAN: I just don't want you talking to him. Is that clear?

CHLOE: Why not? Why is this so important to you?

STAN: Isn't it enough that I said I don't want you to talk to him?

CHLOE: No! It's not enough!

STAN: Don't make me angry.

CHLOE: How can I do that, Stan? How can I not make you angry? Everything I do makes you angry.

STAN: If you left me alone I wouldn't get angry. Leave me alone.

CHLOE: Stan, use your head. How are we going to get through life without me talking to Jim next door or without you talking to Tammy? (*STAN LOOKS AT CHLOE AS IF HE WAS STRUCK WITH A LIGHTNING BOLT. PAUSE. CHLOE EXPECTS STAN TO REACT IN SOME WAY — TO SAY SOMETHING — BUT HE IS SILENT WITH A GUILTY LOOK ON HIS FACE AS IF CHLOE KNOWS SOMETHING, BUT SHE DOESN'T. SHE STUMBLED INTO SOMETHING BY ACCIDENT*) What's the matter with you? What is it with you? Why is it you don't want me to talk to them? There's something there, isn't there? What is it? You aren't jealous, are you? No, it's not jealousy. It's something else. But what?

STAN: I've got to go.

CHLOE: Oh, no! You stay! You stay and talk this out. Now, what is it? It's not jealousy. No. It can't be. I never gave you cause to be jealous. (*PAUSE*) I know. I know what it is. I was too blind to see it. I trusted you because I never had a thought of betraying you. But you — you ... You have always been suspicious of everything I ever did. Where was I when I was gone too long? Who was I talking to? Who was I looking at? It was all in your mind. Your sick, sick mind. (*CHLOE BEATS HIM WITH THE PAPER AND CRIES HYSTERICALLY. SHE HASN'T ROLLED THE PAPER, PLANNING TO BEAT HIM WITH IT. IT IS A SPONTANEOUS OUTBURST DURING WHICH SHE VENTS HER WRATH*) It's Tammy, isn't it? ISN'T IT?

STAN: Honey, I ah ...

CHLOE: Answer me! You with Tammy! How could you?

STAN: It — it just — happened.

CHLOE: Stan, you're sick.

STAN: You don't understand. It's not my fault.

CHLOE: I understand. I finally understand. I understand you very well.

STAN: It — it just — happened.

CHLOE: (*TOTALLY IN CONTROL*) I understand you now, Stan. You finally found a woman who understands you — completely. (*SHE EXITS*)

STAN: You don't understand. Not really, you don't. (*HE EXITS*)

Proper 27
Mark 12:38-44

Single Mom

Theme

The single parent has pressures and stresses that are overwhelming. The church should be helping.

Summary

Sarah, a single mom, is in over her head. The baby is crying, her ex-husband won't send the support check, she is trying to raise a teenage daughter, and is taking a course at the university.

Playing Time	3 minutes
Setting	Sarah's apartment
Props	Phone, a theme paper for class, a storybook
Costumes	Contemporary, casual
Time	The present
Cast	SARAH — mom
	EVIE — her teenage daughter
	TIFF — another daughter, younger

SARAH: (*ENTERS, ON THE PHONE*) Well, you've got to, that's all. I need the money! (*EVIE ENTERS. TO EVIE*) Did you get her to bed?

EVIE: I got her to bed but she's standing up.

SARAH: Standing up!

EVIE: Yes, standing up.

SARAH: Standing up in bed.

EVIE: Right in the middle.

SARAH: Why won't she lie down?

EVIE: She said she won't go to sleep until you "wead her a beddy-bye stowy."

SARAH: I have a report due for statistics class tomorrow.

EVIE: I think she'll fall asleep on her own.

SARAH: Standing up?

EVIE: Sure. Yeah, probably. Oh, I don't know. Go "wead her a beddy-bye stowy."

SARAH: I can't. (*CHANGING HER MIND*) Oh, all right. (*CHANGING HER MIND*) No, I really can't. Can't you read to her?

EVIE: I tried. No, she wants you. She's standing in the middle of the bed waiting for you.

SARAH: Okay, okay. No, I can't leave this report right now. Just let her stand there. At least she's not crying right now.

EVIE: No, not yet she's not. (*TIFF BEGINS TO CRY FOR HER MOM, OFFSTAGE*)

SARAH: (*BACK ON THE PHONE*) What? Oh, Brian, I forgot all about you. Listen, you just better get that money to me, that's all. (*SLAMS PHONE DOWN*) Good-bye, you slime. (*TO EVIE, INDICATING SHE SHOULD GO SEE ABOUT TIFF*) Oh, for goodness sake, could you?

EVIE: Mom, I've got homework to do, too.

SARAH: What am I supposed to do?

EVIE: Go "wead her a beddy-bye stowy."

SARAH: I don't have time.

EVIE: Well, I don't either.

SARAH: Take the time, please, Evie. Please.

EVIE: Aw, Mom, why can't you?

SARAH: Please.

EVIE: Oh, all right. (*SHE BEGINS TO EXIT*) It's like I don't have any of my own work to do. (*SHE EXITS*)

SARAH: Stupid! Stupid! Why did I ever have to take this stupid course? (*THROWING REPORT ON THE FLOOR AND STOMPING ALL OVER IT. THROWING HERSELF ON THE FLOOR AND HAVING A TANTRUM, CRYING AND THEN COLLAPSING LIFELESS ON THE PAPER*)

EVIE: (*ENTERS, STARING AT HER MOM*) Mom? Mom are you...? (*NUDGES HER WITH HER FOOT*)

SARAH: (*RAISING HER HEAD*) What are you doing?

EVIE: (*JUMPING BACK*) What are you doing?

SARAH: What?

EVIE: Mom, I thought ...

SARAH: What?

EVIE: I thought you were dead.

SARAH: Dead? No, I'm not dead. I don't have time to be dead. It's not on the calendar for today. I have a report to do for Professor Winslow's class and it's due tomorrow. After my statistics class, after I pick you up from swimming lessons and after I pick up Tiffany from day care and after I fix dinner and after I put Tiffany to bed and after we eat and after I wash the dishes and after I wash a load of clothes and after I iron your skirt for school for the next day, then we'll see. Yes, then we'll see. Maybe tomorrow I'll have time to be dead. Check back with me tomorrow about this same time.

EVIE: Mom, I'm tired.

SARAH: Welcome to the club.

EVIE: Boy, I can't wait till I grow up.

SARAH: I can't wait until your sister grows up.

EVIE: She might grow up faster since she's still standing in the middle of the bed crying.

SARAH: Let her stand. Let her stand all night. I don't care. (*MORE CRYING FROM TIFF*) No. I do care. Evie, go shut her up somehow.

EVIE: What do you suggest?

SARAH: Read to her.

EVIE: You can't read to her. She's crying.

SARAH: Well, then, take the book and yell it to her.

EVIE: Oh, that's ridiculous.

SARAH: Just do it.

EVIE: All right. I'll do it. (*SHE EXITS*)

SARAH: Now maybe I can get back to this report. (*PICKS UP PAPERS*) Oh, no. I wonder if Professor Winslow will mind if his statistics have chocolate pudding on them. (*TIFF IS CRYING AND EVIE IS YELLING A BOOK TO HER OFFSTAGE. PHONE RINGS. SARAH ANSWERS IT*) I need that money! And I need it right now. I'm warning you, I'm going to call my lawyer! ...What? Oh, who? Oh, Mrs. Snyder. Oh, I'm sorry, Mrs. Snyder. What? The altar guild? No. No. I really don't need anything to occupy my time since my divorce. Thank you so very much. Good-bye.

EVIE: (*ENTERS*) Mom! I can't yell anymore. My throat hurts. (*SARAH BEGINNING TO EXIT*) Mom, did you hear me? Where are you going?

SARAH: I'm going to bed. And I'm going to stand right in the middle of it and cry. (*SHE EXITS*)

Fear

Theme

A time of tribulation is coming, but we sometimes make our own times of tribulation.

Summary

Sam and Rena have had a big fight and Rena walked out threatening divorce. Now they are in the same room but don't see each other. It's the worst time ever at the Pesky home.

Playing Time	3 minutes
Setting	The Pesky home
Props	None
Costumes	Contemporary, casual
Time	The present
Cast	SAM PESKY
	RENA — his wife
	BILL — their son
	TIFF — their daughter

SAM: (*ENTERS*) Rena! Rena!

RENA: (*ENTERS*) Where is Sam? (*NEITHER SAM NOR RENA SEE EACH OTHER*)

SAM: She'll be back. She always comes back.

RENA: I thought he'd be here.

SAM: She's got to come back. She's got to.

RENA: It's just like him to run away from the problem.

SAM: What if she doesn't come back? I guess I wouldn't blame her.

RENA: I don't know how we came to this. It didn't used to be like this.

SAM: She really didn't get much of a bargain when she got me.

RENA: We used to do a lot of things together. A lot of things.

SAM: I'm a loser. A real loser.

RENA: Now he has his interests and I have mine.

SAM: What would I do if she does come back?

RENA: I suppose this had to happen. We were growing apart.

SAM: If she came in right now I'd apologize. Then she'd have to listen to me.

RENA: It might even be for the best. That's what they tell me.

SAM: She'd have to take me back. We could start over.

RENA: When love dies we ought to bury it.

SAM: Things would get back to how they used to be.

RENA: It would never be the same now.

SAM: No, that wouldn't be any good.

RENA: Too much has happened. There's too much that can't be forgiven.

SAM: If things were just like they always were that would be pretty bad.

RENA: Why did it happen?

SAM: Where did things go wrong?

RENA: I guess I've changed.

SAM: I haven't changed so much.

RENA: Sam and I grew apart when I changed and he didn't want to.

SAM: I'm still the guy I was when she married me. Well, maybe that's the problem.

RENA: And he didn't want me to change either.

SAM: I haven't changed. That's the problem.

BILL: (*ENTERS*) I wonder where everyone is?

RENA: And the kids are wild. I can't do anything with them.

SAM: What worries me is the kids. What will happen to them?

TIFF: (*ENTERS*) Mom? Dad? I wonder where ...

RENA: I worry about them so much. I know this is stressful for them both, but I can't do anything about it.

SAM: I should be a better husband. A better father. No doubt about it.

BILL: That's for sure, no one cares what happens to me.

RENA: What am I supposed to do? I know I yell at the kids a lot.

SAM: I hit Bill the other day. I can't even remember why now.

TIFF: I know Mom and Dad are headed for a divorce.

SAM: I need to change. That would change our marriage.

RENA: I'm under a lot of pressure.

BILL: I'm just going to run away.

SAM: I'm scared I can't change.

RENA: I'm fearful.

BILL: Me frightened? Me? No, not me. Not much.

TIFF: I'm terrified. What will happen to me? (*ALL EXIT IN DIFFERENT DIRECTIONS*)

Hosanna!

Theme

We, as church attendees, don't understand what we're doing or what we are saying sometimes. We just go through the paces.

Summary

There are three people in the crowd watching Jesus as he enters Jerusalem. They are enthusiastically yelling "Hosanna." But they have no idea what it means.

Playing Time	3 1/2 minutes
Setting	Jerusalem
Props	None
Costumes	Contemporary, casual
Time	The time of Jesus
Cast	MENE — a person in the crowd
	TEKEL — a friend
	UPHARSIN — and another one

MENE: *(ENTERS ALONG WITH TEKEL AND UPHARSIN)* HOSANNA!

TEKEL: HOSANNA!

UPHARSIN: HOSANNA!

TEKEL: Isn't it wonderful, watching our Messiah enter Jerusalem?

MENE: Wonderful!

TEKEL: It certainly is.

MENE: Hosanna.

UPHARSIN: Hosanna.

MENE: Hosanna. I love to say, "Hosanna."

TEKEL: Hosanna. Me too.

UPHARSIN: Hosanna. Hosanna. Hosanna. It sounds great, doesn't it? I wonder sometimes what it means.

MENE: Me too.

TEKEL: Does it mean something?

MENE: I suppose so.

UPHARSIN: Why else would we be saying it? "Hosanna."

MENE: Why did you say it?

TEKEL: I said it because you did.

UPHARSIN: I heard you saying it, so I did too. It sounds good.

MENE: It does sound good. "Hosanna."

UPHARSIN: Do we have to know what it means? Can't we just say it without knowing what it means?

TEKEL: I say a lot of things I don't know the meaning of, like "Messiah." I have no idea what "Messiah" means. It sounds great and everyone else is saying it.

MENE: So why shouldn't we? Why bother ourselves with the meaning?

TEKEL: Does it mean something?

UPHARSIN: I thought it was just his name or something — "Jesus Messiah." They give children such funny names these days.

TEKEL: It's a nice name.

MENE: Yes, I like it. "Messiah."

TEKEL: We certainly don't need to know what it means. All we're required to do is to say it.

UPHARSIN: That's right. Hosanna, Jesus, Messiah!

TEKEL: Hosanna, Jesus, Messiah!

MENE: Hosanna, Jesus, Messiah!

TEKEL: Hosanna, Jesus, Messiah! (*TO CONGREGATION*) Come on. Say it with us. Come on. It sounds nice.

MENE: Hosanna, Jesus, Messiah!

UPHARSIN: That's right. Hosanna, Jesus, Messiah!

ALL: (*THEY EXIT LEADING THE CONGREGATION IN A CHANT*) Hosanna, Jesus, Messiah! Hosanna, Jesus, Messiah!